A Visioning & Journaling Guide For Caregivers

Creative Healing Through Transformation

Conversations With My Soul

Donna Fitzgerald & Tana Heminsley

Foreword by Diana Reyers
Founder of Daring to Share Global

CREATIVE HEALING THROUGH TRANSFORMATION

CONVERSATIONS WITH MY SOUL

Donna Fitzgerald
&
Tana Heminsley

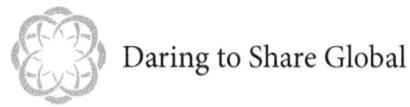 Daring to Share Global

Published by Donna Fitzgerald and Tana Heminsley
February 2021 ISBN: 9781777549503

Copyright © 2021 by Donna Fitzgerald and Tana Heminsley
All rights reserved. No part of this publication may be reproduced, stored in or introduced into a retrieval system, or transmitted, in any form, or by any means (electronic, mechanical, photocopying, recording or otherwise) without the prior written permission of the publisher. This book is sold subject to the condition that it shall not, by way of trade or otherwise, be lent, resold, hired out, or otherwise circulated without the publisher's prior consent in any form of binding or cover other than that in which it is published and without a similar condition including this condition being imposed on the subsequent purchaser.

Editor: Diana Reyers
Typeset: Greg Salisbury
Book Cover Design: Olli Vidal

DISCLAIMER: Readers of this publication agree that, neither Donna Fitzgerald, Tana Heminsley, or Daring to Share Global will be held responsible or liable for damages that may be alleged as resulting directly or indirectly from the use of this publication. Neither the lead publisher nor the self-publishing author can be held accountable for the information provided by, or actions, resulting from, accessing these resources

BY THE AUTHORS

Daring to Share:
8 Brave Souls Sharing Their Authentic Road Trip - Volume 1
Donna Fitzgerald, Contributing Author
Tana Heminsley, Contributing Author

Daring to Share:
There to Here - 2nd Edition | Volume 1
Donna Fitzgerald, Contributing Author
Tana Heminsley, Contributing Author

www.DaringToShare.com

Awaken Your Authentic Leadership: Lead with Inner Clarity and Purpose
Tana Heminsley, Author

Awaken Your Authentic Leadership: Authenticity Journal
Tana Heminsley, Author

Awaken Your Authentic Leadership:
Authentic Leadership Conversations for Meaningful Connection
Tana Heminsley, Author

EASE Amidst Challenging Times:
Simple Practices For Inner Peace Beyond COVID
Tana Heminsley, Author

www.LeadAuthentic.com

IN THANKS

BY DONNA FITZGERALD

To my children Shawn and Shannon, you are my strength and inspiration for writing this workbook. You fill my heart with love and light.

My journey through grief, trauma, and change was not experienced alone. There were many who listened when I needed to speak my truth and who held me up when I was ready to fall. There were and still are those who help push me outside my comfort zone to experience life in a way that brings me laughter, joy, and personal growth.

To my editor, Diana Reyers, thank you for your wisdom, friendship, and support. I am forever grateful for our chance meeting over ten years ago. Little did I know that together we would share so many exciting awakenings within my spiritual journey.

To Tana Heminsley, thank you for trusting and believing in my vision of writing a book for caregivers, allowing me the privilege to adapt your Authentic Leadership Conversation™ worksheets to fit my vision for caregivers while adding my own personal writings through my healing journey.

To my sisters Debbie and Tracy, thank you for your unconditional love, for supporting me throughout my life. You are my place of comfort.

To Robert Gunter, thank you for arriving in my life when I was lost and experiencing chaos. You offered me nothing but love and support even when I stumbled and fell. You have always been and continue to be my biggest supporter.

To TB Turnbull, thank you for your friendship. You have always been available when I needed to talk as I navigated being a single parent, offering help as I created my new life.

Patti Dixon-Medora, thank you for your friendship. For being that friend who says *yes* to all my crazy ideas around trying new activities and being my coffee buddy.

Dr. Michael O'Reilly, thank you for your friendship and support. You introduced me to strength training and triathlons, nudging me outside my comfort zone and reawakening my passion for swimming.

Neuromuscular Clinic team, Kingston, Ontario, Canada, thank you for supporting me while our family lived with ALS. You supported me with my desire to be a volunteer and give back to support ALS families. Thank you for giving me a sense of purpose and the opportunity to be of service while I moved through my own healing.

Thank you to all those who have touched my life over the past twenty years. To all who witnessed and were a part of my incredible journey. I hold everyone within my heart and am grateful for the lessons and the growth we shared.

IN THANKS

BY TANA HEMINSLEY

This book has been a true collaboration – 15 years in the making.

I wrote the foundational book called *Awaken Your Authentic Leadership: Authentic Leadership Conversations for Meaningful Connection*. This book included 18 Action Worksheets for developing skills to become a best-self or authentic organizational leader.

Diana Reyers then adapted the worksheets for an audience outside of the corporate world in our book, *Daring To Share Your Story: An Authentic Writing Guide*.

And Donna Fitzgerald, in our book, *Creative Healing Through Transformation: Conversations with My Soul*, with Diana's guidance and editing support, adapted the worksheets even further in order to support caregivers.

Donna is a self-described quiet person. I would describe her as a humble yet powerful influencer. Her intent to support other caregivers is clear and based on years of personal experience. It has included both the incredible journey to support her husband, Cliff, to live and die with dignity as he faced Lou Gehrig's disease, also known as ALS, as well as her personal journey of discovery and healing from childhood sexual assault.

My *Awaken Your Authentic Leadership* book series, while written for an organizational audience, was also a system I used in order to recover from childhood trauma in my own journey to become my best self.

I am truly grateful to Donna for co-creating this book. My hope is that the ripple effect is global. What would the world do without caregivers? How will the world be healed as they reclaim their authentic selves as they support others and beyond?

Thank you, Donna

DEDICATION

I dedicate this book to my late husband, Cliff.

And to our children, Shawn and Shannon,
you are my greatest gift and inspiration.

TESTIMONIALS

I applaud the authors for this beautiful healing book that could only have been written by someone who has successfully navigated the lived experience of major loss and change in life direction. The frameworks and exercises in this book provide really practical stepping stones for the reader through this difficult and uncharted territory – a route that enables the reader to realize the power of emotional intelligence, spirituality and authenticity to successfully transcend the most profoundly difficult life experiences. I urge anyone who has suffered such a life changing loss to use this highly empowering and insightful guide to navigate towards a place of healing for the mind and soul.

Mike Fitzpatrick, Physician and Chief of Staff, KHSC
Kingston, Ontario, Canada

I am honoured to be asked to write a few words about this workbook, Creative Healing Through Transformation, written by Donna Fitzgerald. I am a Rehabilitation Physician and have spent my career working with individuals and caregivers affected by ALS and other neuromuscular conditions. I witnessed Donna's personal journey through the many stages of providing care for a loved one while still balancing many other roles. All of us in the Neuromuscular Clinic witnessed her adjustment and recovery and we were pleased that she continued to work through the ALS Society as a peer support for other caregivers. Peer support is such a critical part of the supports offered to individuals. Peers bring the lived experience and validation of the broad breath of emotion that caregivers may feel. I am pleased that Donna has written this workbook so that she and others can continue to help caregivers. The workbook shares her personal stories in a way that encourages other to follow the path of healing. It is a wonderfully guided journey, while not being prescriptive, that can be used by individuals, in support networks and with peer support. Thank you Donna for writing and sharing this, I am confident that it will help others.

Karen M. Smith MD
Kingston, Ontario, Canada

Rich Resource Guide. In this rich resource guide, the author provides a practical step by step approach to self-discovery through journaling. With empathy and compassion, she walks alongside the reader, acknowledging the fear and anxiety that may accompany such an introspective journey. She encourages and supports the reader throughout the process, providing useful tips and guidance along the way. By sharing frank and honest insights into her personal story of loss, followed by her journey of self-discovery, self-awareness and renewal, the author provides a unique and authentic voice to the power of journaling. The result is a practical and welcome addition to the toolbox of resources for caregivers across a wide spectrum.

Patti Dixon-Medora, Caregiver Support Group Facilitator,
Alzheimer Society of KFL&A, Kingston, Ontario, Canada

This is an amazing workbook. Well written and simple to follow. The author shows, through personal anecdotes, a courageous journey that will aid others to also take the steps necessary for personal growth. Whether experiencing personal loss and grief or wanting to lead a more authentic and emotionally healthy life, this workbook provides the reader with excellent examples and exercises that can help lead to a richer understanding of ones' Self."

Sylvia Simonyi-Elmer, B.Sc, DCS, RP
Registered Psychotherapist
Kingston, Ontario, Canada

If you are looking for a structured way to help you on your journey to improved self-awareness and the peace that comes with living an authentic life, then this book is for you. Donna and Tana's handbook provides clear and compassionate tools for caregivers to help them re-discover who they are in the face of their role as a caregiver. Each chapter offers descriptions and activities that can be easily incorporated into a caregiver's daily routine. And the pay-off is tremendous – discovering self-awareness; finding your true inner voice and living an authentic life. Donna's honest and, at times, vulnerable journaling is both helpful and uplifting as an example of how using these tools can help a caregiver grow to become the person they are meant to be.

Teresa Whalen
Kingston, Ontario, Canada

I will never forget the first day that we met Donna at the ALS clinic that we were to start attending. I was so overwhelmed by what Maurice and I were facing that I felt like my life now was on a downward spiral. I was angry that he had been diagnosed with this and could not believe it was real.

Donna stood up as we entered the room and Maurice was very charismatic and connected with Donna immediately. After our introduction I remember thinking how lucky we were to have met her because she was answering all of our questions about the unknowns ahead of us in a very calm, honest way and that is what we really needed at this point to face the truth about this disease.

I then remember when she said about her husband having to go to the hospital for care and that he had passed away, it now hit me that this was so real and that the years ahead were going to be a struggle and very difficult.

Donna was our strength getting through the tough days of this horrible disease and I am so thankful for all of her help and just her kindness that she showed us. When I look back at those dark days Donna was someone that I connected to and was such a source of strength and helped us through our journey facing ALS. I will always be thankful for her and we were so blessed to have met her.

Peggy Irvine, Past Caregiver
Kingston, Ontario, Canada

TABLE OF CONTENTS

By The Authors V

Dedication IX

Testimonials X

Conversations XIII

Foreword by Diana Reyers XV

Introduction by Donna Fitzgerald XVII

About Donna Fitzgerald 105

About Tana Heminsley 107

History of Authentic Leadership Global™ 109

Bibliography 111

In Memoriam 112

CONVERSATIONS

Journaling Through Conversation 1:
Understanding Authenticity and Self-Awareness 1

Journaling Through Conversation 2:
Experiencing Your Emotional Feelings 15

Journaling Through Conversation 3:
Living And Journaling Using Your Values For Self-Discovery 23

Journaling Through Conversation 4:
Using Your Inner Purpose Feeling To Connect With Your Soul 37

Journaling Through Conversation 5:
Discovering More About Yourself By Managing Your Inner Critic 47

Journaling Through Conversation 6:
Creating What Inner Balance Feels Like For You 59

Journaling Through Conversation 7:
Setting Boundaries To Express Your Truth 71

Journaling Through Conversation 8, Part 1:
Navigating Transitions Toward The Future 83

Journaling Through Conversation 8, Part 2:
Envisioning The Life You Would Like To Create 97

FOREWORD
BY DIANA REYERS

In January 2012, one week after my husband retired, he was diagnosed with Parkinson's Disease. I remember watching TV with him one evening, and I was distracted when his right foot began tapping the arm of the sofa he was lying on. I quickly realized that the beat of a song was not inspiring his tapping, but that he was experiencing an involuntary tremor he had no control of. I asked him what was going on over there on his side of the room, and he replied that he didn't know, but he had experienced this new phenomenon a couple of times over the past week. At that moment, I felt a surge of adrenaline move through my body; I looked at him and calmly said, *I think you have Parkinson's Disease*.

I will never forget that moment. Since then, for his sake, I have wished many times that it was a nightmare we would wake up from as his life changed forever. When he went to the doctor and received the official diagnosis, the ever-looming unanswered question of what this looks like in 5, 10, or 20 years has ruled his life.

As a classic caregiver, not wanting any of this to be about me, it is uncomfortable to admit that it has also ruled my life as my focus suddenly shifted to doing what I needed to support my husband's quality of life within the progression of his disease. I am grateful I was able to continue working because it provided the distraction I needed to manage the extra emotional capacity required to support the man I vowed to spend the rest of my life with. There is no doubt that the self-work and self-care I committed to was essential to my emotional survival, creating a mindset and way of being that set my husband and me up for success within what we were served - to be able to live alongside his disease, rather than continually fight it.

Being a caregiver, whether as a professional, a partner, child, sibling, or friend, can be a complicated, chaotic cornucopia of added stress, exhaustion, decision-making, guilt, and multi-tasking like you've never mastered before. If you've ever felt like you could absolutely not do one more thing, imagine adding five more to your list and reflect on how that would feel – that is how a caregiver feels most of the time while trying to make it look and feel seamlessly manageable. Love.

I spent the last nine years working relentlessly to maintain the relationship and lifestyle my husband and I always had and dreamed of for the future. The last six years included an adventure, moving to western Canada to explore living in the mountains of the Okanagan and the rain forests of Vancouver Island. Simultaneously, during this time, that my husband's disease progressed, so we decided to return to Ontario where we gravitated to the familiarity of our hometown and feeling of connection being closer to family and life-long friends. We feel blessed to have taken the time to travel because that opportunity will never present again. Acceptance.

If I think of how significantly my life has changed as a caregiver from the day my husband was diagnosed to now, it feels like such a massive and traumatic shift. But, when I break it down into smaller bits using beautiful memories as markers, I realize it transpired as a slow and steady shift that included the love and acceptance I have nurtured in our relationship from the beginning – long before Parkinson's banged our door down.

The key for me was any semblance of ease I could create through the self-awareness I achieved. I needed to understand who I was in order to manage this beast that chose to invade our space. I had a deep knowing that if I understood what felt right for me, I could make decisions that reflected both my husband's and my values. I believe that this is half the battle for many caregivers; both the desire and ambiguity of decision-making within their role of caring for the person they love. It is both an honour and a burden that no one wishes for.

I am grateful that I was introduced to Tana Heminsley and her Conversation series just a year before my husband's diagnosis. This became the added work that saved me. I made room for it, and along with the worksheets, I began a daily practice of journaling and writing.

I was already in a state of feeling stuck for other reasons, so the unplanned timing was perfect. Although it was a shock, by the time my husband received his diagnosis, I was remarkably prepared to add the role of caregiver to my life. Ease.

I won't pretend that it was easy because it was far from it, and this journey is not over yet. However, I can't imagine taking on such an endeavour without the ease of having reached a level of self-awareness to support such a significant undertaking. I am always humbled listening to Donna's story as she shares the inner conflict she experienced moving through her caregiving years. She did not do the work until she experienced burnout four and half years into her caregiving journey. Like so many caregivers, she struggled, moving through the level of adversity that would have broken most; I do not know how she survived and then stepped up to grow and thrive after saying goodbye to the man she loved. She is a warrior amongst humans, particularly as a caregiver who made it through humbly with flying colours.

I did not stop doing the work after my husband's fateful news, and I continue working through this proven self-discovery process with an annual review of the Conversations you are about to delve into. My daily journaling practice is never questioned, providing me with the slowing of time and energy to commit to what Donna so eloquently calls a Conversation With My Soul. It is during this quiet time with myself that I am able to speak my truth, share my woes, and discover the answers I need to continue on my path as an authentic person while, simultaneously being caregiver to my husband.

Whether you want to just dip your toe into some self-awareness or you are ready to dive deep into the pool of self-discovery, Donna and Tana provide you with a process that both validates what you are already sure of while providing you with the amplified confidence you need to support your caregiving journey with acceptance, love, and ease.

INTRODUCTION
BY DONNA FITZGERALD

In the Spring of 2020, the world was faced with the COVID-19 pandemic and stay-at-home restrictions were put in place. I found myself in the at-risk population because I am over sixty. For the next few months, I turned to my self-care routine of meditation and journaling to work through the emotions of my daily routine being interrupted and not being able to visit with family and friends. I started writing and sharing with others how I felt, and I realized that living alone and being isolated awakened my desire to help those also struggling with these changes. I was unclear about what I could do, but I knew I would be guided over time.

I have learned to trust the process and not to rush a particular outcome. During the beginning weeks, I, like hundreds of others, retreated to my kitchen to bake and deliver my goodies to those on the front lines, reaching out to say thank you. I checked in on friends and family every few weeks to let them know I was thinking of them.

For many years I imagined myself writing a book, sharing how I used journaling to connect to my inner voice and soul throughout my caregiving journey. During the isolation of this pandemic, I supported Diana Reyers, my friend, mentor, and publisher of The Daring to Share Global™ series of authentic storytelling books, as she created a program adapting the Authentic Leadership Conversation™ worksheets into a self-discovery writing process. The program was developed to inspire people to become more self-aware while writing their stories as an outlet to share their emotions, awakenings, and personal journey. I met Tana through Diana approximately seven years ago, and eventually became a Facilitator of the Authentic Leadership Conversations™, so I am familiar with the Conversation worksheets created by Tana Heminsley and featured in her Authentic Leadership Global™ book series. I had previously worked through the grief, loss, and trauma experienced from 1998 to 2013. Having found authenticity as a guide to living with more clarity and purpose, I wanted to support those searching for answers within their lives, and I knew that Tana's Conversation worksheets, tools, and practices could provide the help others needed. As a result, I was also inspired to adapt these Conversations into an 8-week program specifically to support caregivers to navigate their supportive role, especially during the added stress of the unprecedented time we were all managing.

I approached Tana to see if she was interested in co-authoring a workbook, adapting her worksheets with the focus on supporting caregivers in the beginning stages of their personal self-discovery journey. I was delighted when she said an emphatic YES! From there, the book started to take shape. While out for a cycle one day this past summer, I was inspired to include some of my free-flow writings at the end of each worksheet, vulnerably sharing the emotions I experienced after my husband's death in 2004. I wanted to include my process of finding myself after caregiver burnout, so those using this book knew there was hope during and beyond their caregiver role.

The timing seemed to be perfect for this adventure as I retried two years ago and always had the desire to make a difference in the lives of others. I found myself wanting to reach out to support caregivers by creating a process they could work through in their own homes while finding answers to the same questions I had, *Who am I? Where do I go from here? What is my purpose? How do I move on?*

Through COVID-19, support groups began meeting online and access to support by family physicians and therapists declined. My hope is that this workbook helps caregivers start a new daily practice of journaling, promoting life-long self-care. At the same time, they will discover more about their authentic self while working through each worksheet at their own pace, taking time to sit with their emotions and awakenings, inspiring more self-awareness. This workbook is a tool to help caregivers begin their personal work as they move through grief and loss. It is a starting point to share their discoveries with a therapist or within a book club or facilitated support group. As individuals, they can create the best environment for themselves to meet their own needs. They will experience the beauty of finding the courage to challenge false messages they have been living with. And they will re-discover the beauty of life that comes with the new unlocked awareness birthed from a different perspective. They will be encouraged to take the time to go within and learn how their values can support their decision-making, how they can manage their inner critic, and discover what inner balance means to them, along with many more insights. My hope is that every caregiver learns the importance of early self-care and realizes the importance of being first on their list, knowing that the stronger they are, emotionally, physically, and spiritually, the longer and more effectively they can support their loved one.

In September 1998, my husband was diagnosed with ALS, and for the next six years, we fought this disease with all we had. He died in November 2004 with dignity and there was nothing unsaid between us. I dedicate this book to his strength, determination, humour, and his love of family, including our children. Without their love, I would not be the woman I am today, sharing my personal reflections throughout this workbook. Within our journey, I found myself making a pledge that I would help families going through what I did, not feel as alone as I did. We had a young family, and there was no one I knew who had children dealing with my reality at the time of my husband's diagnosis. For eight years, I supported ALS families in my area by attending our community's Neuromuscular Clinic, where patients were seen, as well as creating a caregiver group in my home. I also felt honoured that families invited me into their homes and lives to help support them in any way I could. I had lived their reality, so I understood their uncertainty, pain, and frustrations. Unfortunately, at the time, I was not aware of the importance of self-care and eventually found myself in burnout, along with experiencing a deep sense of loss of self. I was only aware of all the roles I played in life. I did not know Donna; she disappeared. It was a terrifying place to be.

Within my desire to support others, I overlooked the fact that, along with a caregiver group, I moved ALS back into my home. My daughter was only eleven when her father died, and she was not moving through her grief very well. My focus became trying to support her through her healing. My son was eighteen and away at college, coping the best way he could, starting his life away from home. From about 1990 to the present day, I have been journaling, processing my emotions, feelings, and having a conversation with myself every day. I find this daily ritual the greatest gift I can give myself. This is how the title of this book came to be. *Creative Healing Through Transformation* is about the creative process of journaling and visioning. The *Conversations With My Soul* are the writings I kept along the way and continue to write when a thought or experience inspires me.

This book, the lessons, and the gifts that lie within its pages will allow you to be still and take the *time* you need to be re-introduced to your soul, the voice that lies deep within your being. It is the voice that has sat silent for so long. You have received a catalyst, awakening a desire to find out what lies beneath the surface without looking to the outside world for answers – the answers that lie deep within you. There may be duplication in the journaling you do. This is normal and it is important to write about what needs to come out for as long as it takes until it shifts to different insights. The courage and vulnerability to commit to the work will awaken you to authenticity, and self-care will become a gift that continues to support you to grow. Life becomes amazing as you move forward, acknowledging, experiencing, and feeling grief, pain, and loss. You can create the ability to face every day with a new perspective and curiosity about what is ahead. Even when life presents challenges, you have the ability to grow with them and with more ease, using the tools and practices that motivate you to answer the questions that create the action required to support you on your path to awesomeness.

OPENING THOUGHTS BY DONNA FITZGERALD

When I began my journaling practice years ago, I was inspired to write additional free-flow *reflections*. After each Conversation in this workbook, I will share a piece of these writings to provide you with additional inspiration as you make your way through this new-found process of having *Conversations with Your Soul*.

Grief is a small word that entered my life with my husband's diagnosis of ALS. It's a sneaky word that slowly crept into my world, grabbing hold while inviting it's friend Fear along for the ride. It was subtle at first. I knew and experienced disappointment and hurt throughout my life but was never introduced to this bad boy.

I started grieving a little at a time as I became a caregiver, nurse, and therapist to my husband; the loss of life as I knew it, future dreams, and my daily life as a partner and wife. Grief got stronger and knocked me to the mat. I was dazed and confused as I tried to get my footing again. Every time I tried to stand, I got knocked back down while Grief said, No you don't; I am here to teach you.

The next one was a knock down punch. I disappeared and lost myself when the door to the awareness of my childhood sexual abuse and the death of my husband opened all at once. Wow! This dude called Grief was serious and deadly. It was determined to keep me in the darkness, out of breath, weak, and a loser.

Little did Grief know that I had superpowers called Healing and Love. With stars in my eyes and the breath knocked out of my body and soul, I saw a little light that meant Hope. I fought through the darkness to stand up and triumph over Grief. I was bloody and bruised but I would not allow Grief to take me away from my children or myself. I chose to fight to live and love. It did not know my strength.

The secret to my victory was fighting to stay in the light of Love for myself and those who touch my life. My loving heart knows the depth of darkness that provides me with the strength to face Grief and life, and say, not today. I am Healing, and there is no room for Grief on my journey into the future I am creating that includes a life with more meaning, purpose, and sunshine.

Along with this awareness, I have the privilege and honour of carrying with me the strength and love of my husband's fight to keep me on my feet even when I am knocked off balance sometimes. I am grateful for and welcome the sunshine of a new day.

Understanding Authenticity and Self-Awareness

Journaling Through Conversation 1

Discover how self-awareness supports living a life that is true to your inner voice - your soul.

How can being self-aware support you on your path to self-discovery?

The following worksheet will assist you in becoming more aware of your inner voice -your soul; to live a life in line with who you are, authentically.
It will also support you to take the first steps to begin journaling and awaken to your authentic self while providing you with a lifelong practice, supporting inner growth.

Things to Consider To Understand Authenticity and Self-Awareness:

- There are several internal and external characteristics associated with being authentic;
- Self-Awareness supports authenticity in several ways;
- Authentic people with strong self-awareness are more confident and decisive;
- Self-Aware people become influencers when modelling their authentic selves;
- Self-Aware people are successful and sustainable over the long term;
- Self-Aware people positively impact their community and world;
- Journaling will support you to cultivate self-awareness, moving you towards a more authentic way of being;
- The Arc of Intense Energy is a tool that supports self-awareness.

There are several internal and external characteristics associated with being authentic:

- Being honest and consistent in all areas of your life;
- Being able to choose the most authentic response in each moment in line with your beliefs and values;
- Creating time to be still, journal, and reflect on thoughts of judgement, assumptions, stories, and perceptions;
- Learning to allow and acknowledge emotional feelings that bubble to the surface, rather than pushing them down when experiencing discomfort;
- Using your intuition – your inner voice/soul - to sense what you really want to say;
- Being able to make daily changes that feel more in line with your self-awareness.

Externally, People Who Live Authentically:[1]

- Are confident and connected to their inner voice;
- Attract others to them by being naturally confident and approachable;
- Remain grounded by being comfortable asking for help and being vulnerable;
- Are consistent in all parts of their life.

Internally, People Who Live Authentically:

- Demonstrate a passion for their purpose;[2]
- Are aware of their impact on others;
- Are aware of their automatic patterns, beliefs, and habits that may inhibit them from being themselves;
- Ask for feedback from others to support them to continue developing awareness;
- Seek both intuitive and logical perspectives from others to support their decision-making.

How would you describe who you are as your authentic self at this point?

---

[1] Adapted from Bill George, Peter Sims, et al., Discovering Your Authentic Leadership, Harvard Business Review, February 2007.
[2] Bill George, "Authentic Leadership: Rediscovering the Secrets to Creating Lasting Value, as cited by Bill George, et al. in Ibid, 2003.

Self-Awareness supports authenticity in several ways:

- When people are self-aware, they have more choice in how they manage situations. They can choose to step back and move beyond their normal, default ways of managing conversations and relationships - particularly when a new response is required. They can respond in a way that resonates with their authentic way of being;
- Self-aware individuals call on their values and their awareness of their strengths and weaknesses to successfully navigate new or stressful situations;
- Self-aware people motivate and engage others as they take the time to build strong relationships through listening and understanding other people's perspectives;
- Self-aware people integrate their personal life with their careers and create environments respectful of both personal values and professional needs. They are more comfortable and successful as a result of their authenticity in all parts of their lives, more of the time - they are consistently the same person in more and more situations.

Daniel Goleman's article, *What Makes a Leader?* introduced a model of emotional intelligence that includes the following five skills. This model is useful as a starting definition for everyone, and understanding it enables people to step into their authenticity to move forward on the path to self-discovery. These include:

- Self-awareness - Knowing one's emotions, strengths, weaknesses, drivers, values, and goals and their impact on others;
- Self-regulation - Controlling or redirecting disruptive emotions and impulses;
- Motivation - Being driven to achieve for the sake of achievement; also balancing external with internal, intrinsic motivations;
- Empathy - Considering others' emotional feelings, especially when making decisions;
- Social Skill - Managing relationships to move people in desired directions.[3]

How self-aware do you feel you are currently? Can you describe a time when you needed to intentionally tap into one of the five listed skills of self-awareness to manage a situation in an authentic way?

---

[3] Daniel Goleman, "What Makes a Leader?" Harvard Business Review, 1998.

Authentic people with strong self-awareness are more confident and decisive:

- Build trust-based relationships as individuals who see and shift old patterns limiting them from connecting with others;
- Resolve challenges before they become a problem and become better active listeners. As a result, they are more open to possibilities, less defensive, and more available and able to have difficult conversations;
- Show up with grounded confidence, which creates a more stimulating and engaging environment for them and those around them;
- Able to manage the increasing volume and complexity of life demands because they can maintain perspective, cultivate ease, and focus their efforts on what is deeply important to them at that time;
- They practice developing balance by adjusting their schedule, priorities, and the way they engage with others in order to be consistently rejuvenated versus being exhausted;
- They also discover how to shift and maintain balance of inner self in order to create a calmer way of being.

Self-Aware people become influencers when modelling their authentic selves:

- Being around authentic people inspires positivity as others can be vulnerable with them because they are approachable and available;
- Others know where they stand on a day-to-day basis with someone who is being authentic (rather than walk on eggshells because they are unsure how they will react), and this creates the confidence needed to have difficult conversations;
- Self-aware individuals can engage more effectively as they build the skill to involve others and let go of old patterns of micro-managing and control.

Self-Aware people are successful and sustainable over the long term:

- Self-aware people can make authentic decisions with clarity as they welcome a variety of opinions and encourage meaningful conversation. They are not as hasty to make decisions before considering different perspectives;
- They decrease risks and increase transparency as they can ask for help when they need it versus trying to deal with issues on their own. For some people, this can provide a profound shift.

Self-Aware people positively impact their community and world:

- Self-aware people create a win-win-win situation for others and themselves in all areas of their life and the world as they follow their authentic passion;
- They create environments where everyone involved can be themselves and feel safe to approach others in difficult situations. The ripple effect moves outside of themselves to their community and the rest of the world.

How do you feel trusting and tapping into your self-awareness more often would change your life?

How do you think this would change the lives of those you interact with and the rest of the world?

The Arc of Intense Energy is a tool that supports self-awareness:

When you are unaware of your thoughts and emotions, at the peak of the Arc of Intense energy, your body cannot tolerate the discomfort, and your mind will do anything to resolve the tension. Often this means reacting using old, unhelpful automatic patterns of thoughts and behaviors to deal with situations. Remember a time when you lashed out at someone and afterwards wished you would not have said what you did. These situations involve being on the *Arc*.

When you practice cultivating awareness, on the other hand, you navigate with that inner guidance system. You can begin by paying attention; noticing the energy or discomfort intensifying in the body. As this occurs, practice relaxing your shoulders and belly and deepen and slow your breathing. This will allow you to feel the emotions as they arise, notice your thoughts and discern if they are aligned with your values or just old, unhelpful messages. When you learn to discern which is true and right for you, you will be able to maintain your perspective and choose an appropriate and authentic response for the situation at hand.

This is an advanced skill found in an emotionally mature and authentic individual and takes time and practice to master. Take the time now to review the Arc of Intense Energy.

Creative Healing Through Transformation

The Arc of Intense Energy:

During stressful situations, your body will go into fight, flight or freeze. When this occurs, it can be difficult to stay present to your thoughts and emotions that start when you are triggered and feel like a wave of intense energy that builds and builds, and eventually dissipates. This experience is depicted below as an *Arc*. It can occur within seconds.

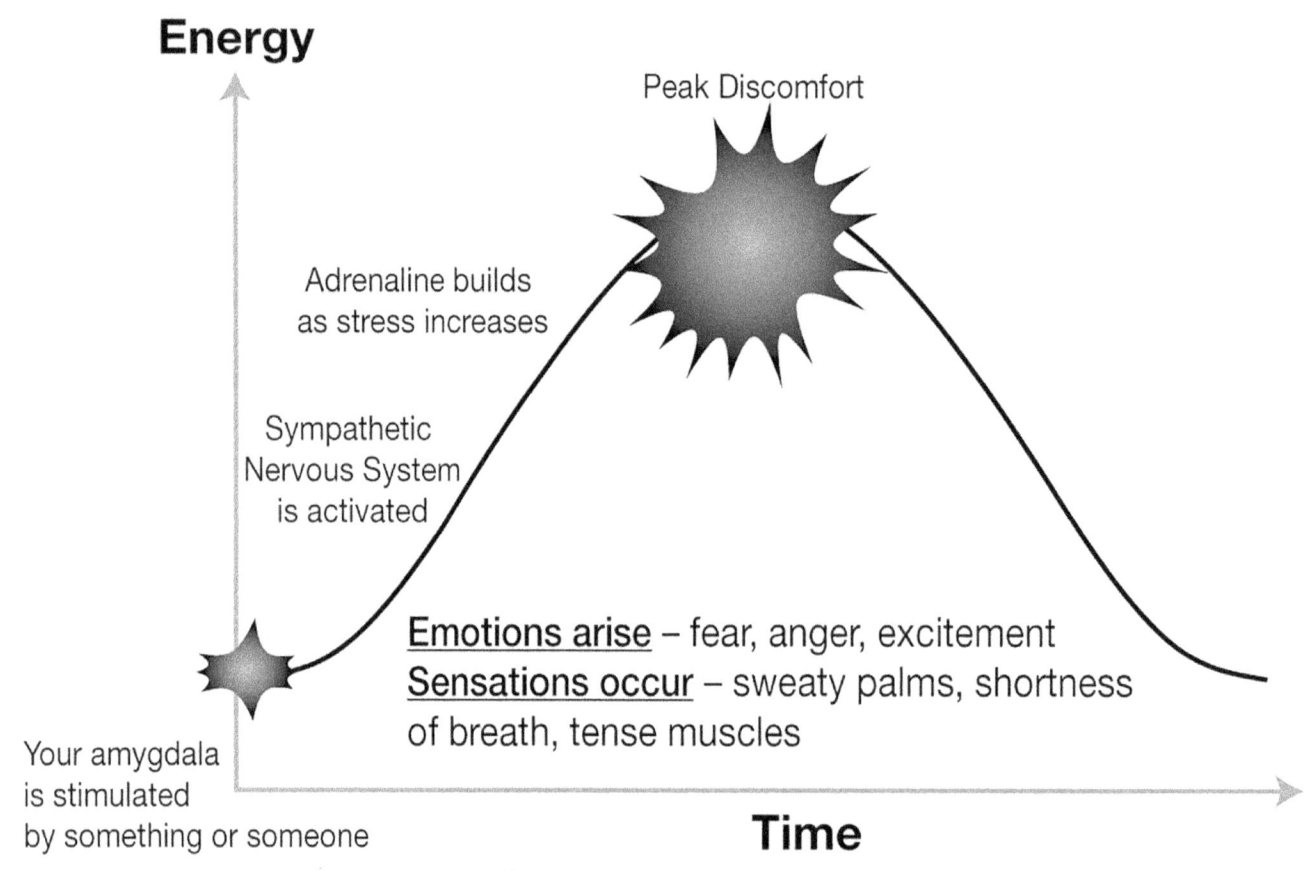

Arc of Intense Energy Reflection:

Reflect on the topic of this Conversation – *Understanding Authenticity and Self-Awareness*. Answer the following questions in order to understand how the *Arc* is showing up for you:
What is your old, automatic pattern when triggered? For example, *When I am triggered by a person who I feel is aggressive towards me. I begin to feel my heart race and my breathing changes; I then hold my breath and shut down:*

What is a new behaviour, belief, or attitude you would like to choose instead? For example, *When I am triggered by a person who I feel is being overly aggressive towards me, I take a deep breath, recognize the physical change within my being, then take a moment to gather my thoughts so I can speak in a calm, non-defensive manner. When I was a caregiver for my husband in the later stages of his ALS diagnosis, he needed full care, was in a wheelchair, and unable to speak. During the last eighteen months of his disease, when I brought him home on weekends from the long-term care facility, he was frustrated and angry. The only way he could express his frustration was by lashing out at me by running into me with his wheelchair or making loud sounds. Initially, I reacted by getting angry and having an argument with him. Over time, I learned to take a deep breath, remove myself from the situation and come back into the room when he felt less aggressive. I was able to have a conversation with him and find out exactly what his frustration was and how I could help him get the support he needed:*

After a few weeks of practicing, reflect on what you are learning and how you will adjust your thoughts and behaviors as a result.

Journaling will support you to cultivate self-awareness, moving towards a more authentic way of being:

The basis for practicing self-awareness through daily journaling with the intention to be more authentic is that you commit to finding ways to learn about yourself, including what motivates and challenges you and *who* you are when living from authentic intention.

I was introduced to journaling twenty years ago while struggling with the demands of caring for my husband with Lou Gehrig's disease, otherwise known as ALS, working full time, and raising my family. I started therapy to help navigate the emotions, fears and thoughts that became part of my life. The therapist suggested journaling. I discovered that writing was the greatest gift I gave myself twenty years ago as it provided me with the ability to maintain a conversation with my soul, my inner voice, every day.

Steps to Self-Awareness Through Daily Journaling:

- In the beginning stages of journaling, please be gentle with yourself and have an open mind;
- It takes time to feel comfortable with this new daily tool as it guides you towards living a more authentic life while being more self-aware;
- Create a quiet spot away from the noise of the world, a room that includes a comfortable chair, side table, and light;
- Shut the door and ask those in your life to not disturb you; in time, this will become a very sacred space where you feel secure in revealing your emotions and thoughts in your journal;
- Choose a time of day that fits your schedule and becomes a regular practice built into daily life;
- Use a journal or pad of paper;
- Once you are comfortable, take a few deep breaths, releasing any tension you may be holding in your body;
- At the beginning, just journal for ten minutes. You may not be used to sitting still while writing your thoughts down on paper. This may feel a lot longer. Hang in there!
- Initially, you may feel confused, silly, and even blank on what to write down. It takes practice to sit down and quiet a mind that is used to going all the time;
- Journaling involves writing down thoughts that come to you naturally. In the beginning, it may just be a list of things you need to do that day. Or, it may be writing down how you feel at that moment. For example, *This is ridiculous*;
- You will find that thoughts and emotions come easier over time if you are patient and stick with the process;
- Journaling does not need to make sense; the intention is not to tell a story or follow a certain flow. It is simply about writing down any thought that enters your consciousness;
- As you start and continue this process, various emotions may come to the surface - anger, frustration, fear. Acknowledging these emotions will allow you to begin releasing what has been hidden in your subconscious;
- You may feel yourself experience the Arc of Intense Energy (review above); this is an opportunity for you to practice taking a deep breath, sitting for a moment, and then asking yourself questions to help understand and reveal why you feel this way. For example, *Why do I feel this emotion? What memory is coming up with the emotion?*
- Keep it simple and continue to write what comes to you.

Action Steps

Exercise:

- Determine your personality type by completing The Enneagram Institute Personality Test at https://tests.enneagraminstitute.com or the short version in the book The Wisdom Of The Enneagram: The Complete Guide to Psychological and Spiritual Growth for the Nine Personality Types by Don Richard Riso and Russ Hudson. This information will support you to be more self-aware and understand your developed personality and who you are as your authentic and best self. You will also discover what your personality looks like as it's unbalanced self and use this information as you move through your self-discovery process. You will be amazed at how accurate the Enneagram is at explaining the personality you have developed over time;
- Review the Arc of Intense Energy described above, and be open to noticing times you may feel yourself entering the *Arc* during uncomfortable, indecisive situations and around certain people, while at your workplace, and during your journaling process. Be curious about what you are uncomfortable with and slow your breathing down to give yourself space to notice and gather your thoughts to determine your next move, what you want to say and how you want to be. This will support you to shift when you are sharing about people and situations that trigger you towards reactions that don't serve you well.

Reflections:

- By utilizing tools like The Enneagram Personality Test, The Arc of Intense Energy, and daily journaling, reflect on what you are learning about living an authentic life with new self-awareness. What are you discovering about who you are as your authentic self? Write your thoughts here:

- Have you experienced any new awareness through your journaling?

- Are you more aware of emotions arising? Do you find yourself listening to your inner voice, your intuition or soul, and as a result, choosing to make small changes towards being more authentic? If so, what are they?

- After learning more about your Enneagram personality characteristics, are you surprised how much you resonate with this personality type? Describe how you would articulate your personality today?

Now it's time to discover more about yourself through journaling:

- Journaling is the foundation to help you embark on your journey of self-discovery. The practice of daily journaling will provide time to have a conversation with your soul. It will allow you to speak without the fear of others reading your words and being upset with what you write and feel. It will provide you with the freedom to listen to what you need from your inner self, rather than what others expect from the outside world;
- Journaling can be uncomfortable initially as you uncover a lifetime of patterns, memories, and experiences buried deep within your subconscious. You may feel a floodgate of emotions as you allow them to come to the surface and become more self-aware. These feelings and thoughts need to flow in order for you to continue to discover your authentic self. In the beginning, what you write may not make sense, but that's okay; stick with the process;
- Journaling can be the tool that supports you towards being more self-aware and authentic. There is no right or wrong to journaling, and you will discover what works for you. Use your pen and paper to experience the creative aspect of journaling. Let free-flow thinking travel into your pen, placing your thoughts onto the blank page in front of you. You may use questions to guide you through the process every day. For example, *How am I feeling? Why do I feel this emotion when I experience....? Why am I so anxious? What is causing my anger?*
- You can also include a practice of journaling with coloured pens, choosing a colour each day that represents how you feel. Use colours that make you feel happy on days that seem to flow with ease, and other colours that resonate with days that feel darker and stressful, or when you are feeling angry or frustrated;
- You are the creator behind your journaling, and there is no need to edit your words. You will find that starting with writing a general daily *to-do* list or what happened the day before will naturally take you to a writing flow, moving you to deeper thoughts with more meaning. Continue to write as long as thoughts stream onto the page;

- When you stop journaling that day, review your writing and contemplate what your thoughts mean to you. This may inspire your next journaling session or a change in your life that reveals itself though that day's writing reflection;
- Your journal entries are for your eyes only. You may choose to keep them in a safe place to review later – to see where you were at any given time. Or, you may choose to burn them once they are full as a ritual of letting go of what was revealed. It is your personal choice to do what feels good for you as this is your new journey of self-discovery;
- If you have someone in your life who you trust and feel guided to share what your journaling reveals, this may help you gain clarity and have support as you move forward;
- If you find you are overwhelmed by what comes up for you and need additional support, please seek a therapist, counsellor, or coach to safely help you;
- Make sure to eat before, during, or after journaling.

Daily Practices to Support Self-Discovery Through Journaling:
These are recommended practices; I encourage you to find those that resonate with you.

- Commit to daily foundational practices and choose what resonates with you: eating well, including hydrating; rest, including sleep and taking time to slow down during the day; movement, including exercise, stretching, or yoga; add the free-flow activity of walking on your own in nature to stimulate the right side of your brain;
- Take your phone with you while walking – not to make calls or text, but to capture thoughts that arise. You will find that the right side of your brain will become ignited, and incredible insights will pop up!! Record any thoughts or emotions that bubble up and that you may want to include in your story;
- Meditate or provide space to lay and be still before getting out of bed in the morning. This is a lovely quiet few moments that allows your soul to wake up before beginning your day;
- Then, sit up on the side of your bed, place your feet on the floor and ask yourself, *What will my day be like today?* Give yourself a moment to clarify how you are feeling, emotionally or physically, so you can determine what you can invite into your day. *Did you sleep well? Are you well-rested? Is there some emotional stuff weighing you down? Are you clear-headed? Is your schedule at a low, medium or high capacity?* Clarify anything you need to recalibrate before determining your level of capacity within each piece of your whole self - physical, mental, emotional, and spiritual;
- As you begin daily journaling, start with a moment of gratitude as your first entry.

Congratulations on starting your new path of living with more self-awareness as you discover a life of purpose through journaling. It will support you to become more mindful about being more authentic as you move through difficult transitions such as grief, a career transition, ill-health, and more. This is the first step to revealing who you are through the process of self-awareness and authenticity.

What's Next? Have a Conversation With Your Soul Through Journaling:

What is your soul saying to you about who you are as your authentic self? How are you feeling about emotional intelligence, and how can you express this through journaling – having a conversation with your soul? Grab your journal and write what you are discovering about yourself.

A Conversation With My Soul

By Donna Fitzgerald

Writing is Freedom

Sitting here with pen and paper, I realize that writing has been a gift of freedom for me in my life. My journey to freedom started 15 years ago when I was lost and burnt out from caregiving. I tried to make sense of my husband's death, as I also faced the reality of my childhood abuse. When I started to journal, I began healing from loss and grief. Out of the journaling came the awareness that fear had many faces.

Throughout my childhood, I was afraid people would discover my secret about being sexually abused. Of course, at that age, I didn't know this; it presented itself by me being extremely shy, feeling awkward, and ugly.

As my teenage years approached, I was afraid of joining groups or sports in high school for fear of failure and being laughed at. I feared being noticed and was very insecure, which made me a target for being teased by the boys at school.

As a wife and mother, I tried to be perfect and the best I could be for fear of not measuring up. I felt like I had nothing to say. I knew my place in the adult world and what others expected of me.

Writing gave me a voice and an opportunity to dig deep and acknowledge the feelings, emotions, and thoughts buried inside me. I was lost as I coasted through life being driven by fear. My commitment to writing and facing that fear was the only way I could walk towards freedom and find my personal truth.

Over the years, I wrote thousands of pages, some becoming wet from my tears, and others ripped through my anger, fear and uncertainty of life. Sometimes, I expressed my mood with colors like purple, pink, and orange. I don't go back and read my journals or stories – I like to burn them, which has become a ritual of letting go and moving forward.

Writing has become my daily joy. It is simple yet powerful. Along with that extreme joy, there is deep hurt and pain that comes along with my writing. However, the sense of self-awareness and freedom I receive is worth exposing all my truth. Writing has allowed me to give the little girl within the voice to grow from fear and meet the wonderful woman I am today. That little girl does not need to be protected anymore because she has grown into a strong, confident woman. My journey of words has allowed a pathway to truth and acceptance.

Writing has given me a voice, purpose, and understanding of who I am and my life's journey. I can express myself through words and feel the emotion that each word ignites within my soul. I know that my writing can be like medicine to others and inspire them by sharing my experiences.

Writing has allowed me to love who I am, and I can look in the mirror and love the woman looking back at me because of the courage and determination I had to find Donna.

I allowed my heart to open and let love flow through my pen to discover more about myself and life. I am blessed!

Experiencing My Emotional Feelings

Journaling Through Conversation 2

Visualize how you feel emotionally and what messages these emotions provide.

What emotions are you experiencing at this time in your life?

The following worksheet will support you to create a visual story revealing what you may be subconsciously feeling. This collage process, along with your newly found daily practice of self-discovery through journaling, will support you to articulate your life now.
This creative activity can be very revealing and provide you with any additional awareness you may need to find clarity and move forward.
An Emotional Feeling Board is a visual picture of how you feel within a transition you may be experiencing. Use it to interpret how you are feeling emotionally and partner it with journaling to create a deeper understanding of how you are currently showing up in your life.
As you develop an awareness of where you are at this moment, you will understand the emotional feelings that surface in your collage and
describe them through the process of writing in your journal.

Things To Consider To Experience Your Emotional Feelings:

- Gather items you need to create your board;
- Prepare a relaxing space that provides ease away from daily stressors;
- Move through a mindful, sensory process guided by your intuition, your soul;
- Review what you learned about authenticity and what it means to you externally and internally;
- Reflect on the awakenings that occur as you review your board;
- Interpret your reflections through your journaling practice;
- Summarize how you feel emotionally after moving through the process of creating and interpreting your board.

Gather items you need to create your board:

- A canvas or poster board;
- A magazine; yes, just one! I prefer using an Oprah magazine as it is full of images, colours, and words;
- A glue stick or liquid glue;
- A sealer medium like Mod Podge; I prefer *matte* as opposed to *shiny*;
- Separate piece of paper and your journal.

Prepare a relaxing space that provides ease away from daily stressors:

- Put on your most comfortable clothing, finding a space that allows for the energy you need to create;
- Put your favourite music on – it may be easy listening, or it may be upbeat – play what inspires you, or no music at all if that resonates;
- Light a scented candle if this is something you enjoy or an unscented one for ambiance;
- Set your canvas or poster board on the table in front of where you will be sitting;
- Give yourself one hour to create your Emotional Feeling Board.

Move through a mindful, sensory process guided by your intuition, your soul:

- Begin looking through your magazine, trusting your intuition as you choose images that resonate with you – avoid trying to justify why you are choosing them; it may be a colour or a memory that comes up, or an item you are drawn to, or it may be a series of words or phrases – decide only based on a positive emotional response you experience;
- Rip out images that resonate with you for whatever reason – pleasant or not, avoiding the use of scissors as they motivate perfectionism and detract from the sensory experience of ripping the paper – *feel* the paper and *listen* to it rip as you use the index finger of your non-dominant hand to guide the paper along while using your dominant hand to pull the paper up and around that finger;
- Put a dab of glue on the image and intuitively find a place directly on your canvas or poster board once ripped out – avoid making a pile of images to choose from later. Instead, place each on the spot on your board as soon as you choose it and rip it out of the magazine. Trust this process as it is based on how you feel and where the image is meant to be from the moment you place it down. Trust your emotions;
- Once you have gone through the magazine, flip through the pages once more to see if anything else resonates that you may have missed. Don't worry if your canvas or poster board is not completely filled as white space reflects emotions you may not have
- investigated yet or been curious about. Your board may end up having more images than words or vice versa, or it may have a combination of both;
- Write your name and the date on the back of the board, so you remember when you created it.

Action Steps

Exercise:

Review what you learned about authenticity and what it means to you externally and internally:

- Once your board is complete, go back to Chapter 1 and review what you learned about authenticity, what it means to you externally and internally. Also review the Arc of Intense Energy and your Enneagram results. Take the time to read the description of your personality type based on these learnings;
- Use what you learned above and review your Emotional Feeling Board, experiencing the somatic sensations that arise in your body and the emotional feelings that arise from your soul. Both of these responses reflect whether your images reflect your authentic self or not. For example, *are you feeling at ease, or are you feeling anxious? If at ease, the emotions you are experiencing reflect your authentic self. If you are feeling anxious, you are likely on the Arc of Intense Energy. Take a moment to reflect on why this might be.*

Reflect on the awakenings that occur as you review your board:

Sit with a pen and your separate piece of paper and review what is revealed. Write the date and what you feel as you experience your board. What do the themes and images represent? Were you drawn to a specific colour, phrase, or image? Why? Do you feel your board is expressing more about where you are now than you thought it would? For example, *Because my board is void of people and colour, I realize I am lost within my grief and caregiver burnout.*

This is the first step to recognizing how you feel emotionally today. It is your starting point in finding clarity about who you are at this time, within what you are experiencing. As you move forward with this series of worksheets, more clarity will arise. For example, *I remember creating my first Emotional Feeling Board a year after my husband died. My board revealed only words and phrases with no colour. I was spending a lot of time journaling and working through the grieving process. This was revealed because I was still healing and had not introduced people into my life or thought about the future for a very long time. A year later, I created another Emotional Feeling Board, and it was very different, including colour and images of people, books, and coffee mugs. It exuded joy because I was opening up to a new awareness and self-discovery.*

Reflections:

Interpret your reflections through your journaling practice:

This sample list of emotional feelings will help you as you interpret your Emotional Feeling Board. You may feel an emotion arise that connects with a thought or memory while you journal your feelings, describing your collage.

Anger	Hope
Amazement	Insecurity
Confusion	Loneliness
Depression	Overwhelm
Disgust	Sadness
Excitement	Surprise
Fear	Trapped
Happiness	Uncomfortable
Helplessness	Worthless

Ask yourself the following questions as you reflect. Notice how it feels and what arises for you in terms of emotions and thoughts. Write down the interpretations you are experiencing in your journal.

- How do I feel right now?
- What do I notice about my thoughts?
- What emotions are arising?
- What was this experience like for me?
- What am I learning about myself as a result?

Notice how it feels practicing being vulnerable within your journaling. How does it feel setting a new daily practice expressing yourself honestly and authentically through your writing?

Summarize how you feel emotionally after moving through the process of creating and interpreting your board:

On your separate piece of paper, step back from your board, and write a description of the emotional feelings that come up. Let the words naturally flow.

As you move through this workbook, the intention is to become more aware of your authentic-self and understand who you are. You will create another board later in Journaling Through Conversation 8, and it will become your new marker of self-discovery. You will see how far you evolve compared to where you are now after experiencing the same self-awareness process.

Example:

Below is a sample of one of my emotional feeling boards and how I describe the emotions I experienced while creating it:

I completed this Emotional Feeling Board after I worked through the grief of losing my husband. I was starting to create a new life for myself with a new connection to my soul. The colors represent joy and hope for my future. I was stepping into new experiences that were scary and exciting at the same time. I had found my voice as depicted by the words and statements on the board. I finally found beauty and happiness after the darkness.

Continued Daily Practices to Support Articulating Your Emotions Through Journaling:

Review the foundational practices suggested at the end of Conversation 1. If you feel comfortable with all of them, continue including them in your daily routine. However, if you are not resonating with one or more, take the time to discover what you prefer practicing to create a mindset that promotes physical, emotional, and spiritual presence.

Stick with daily walking as your free-flow activity. If you have space, feel free to add a different activity or switch it out for another like reading.

What's Next? Have a Conversation With Your Soul Through Journaling:

What is your soul saying to you about how you are experiencing your emotional feelings right now, and how can you express this through journaling – having a conversation with your soul? Grab your journal and write what you are discovering about yourself.

A Conversation With My Soul

By Donna Fitzgerald

The writing below was written nine years after my husband's death.
I have spent these years healing and becoming more connected with my soul and the world around me.

I look in the mirror into the eyes of a woman I have had glimpses of but have not known intimately until now. I say I love you, you are beautiful, you are worthy, and you are love. I smile and say thank you. I like what I see. I am me!

I am aware of my values used to live my life of calm. I am true to myself when I am helping and giving of myself to others. I love spending time with friends and family. I know the importance of not taking my health and mobility for granted and managing my finances to support myself.

I am a woman who enjoys high heels and dresses, feeling beautiful. I believe in myself and need no one to tell me I am beautiful. I am a woman who lives from her heart. I face every day with gratitude and faith that I am where I need to be.

I have found my voice, and with my voice comes confidence and empowerment. To be awakened to the beauty of who I am is amazing. All the thoughts and feelings of being ugly, nothing to say, of being unworthy, are untrue. Although I slip back into these thoughts at times, I know how to acknowledge and let them go.

My purpose in life is to be calm. I know that I can't be calm all the time, but even in the chaos of the day or times of health problems, by sitting with myself and connecting to my inner self, I find calm even when the outside world is not.

I am happy with the simple things in life like a home that speaks to my soul and food on the table to share with family and friends. I am grateful for the ability to stay active, treat my body well, and help others who have experienced a life-changing event; one that has been a catalyst to wanting to know about themselves and answer the question, is there more?

I am growing spiritually and personally every day. I am living in the moment and know that the past is gone; the future is yet to come. I have the now and can feel, take in, and learn from every moment.

I have found my calm and inner peace. I can face the challenging times, knowing they will not last forever; there is light in every day.

I found myself, and I love who I am, and I am proud of what I have done in my life. I accept all of me. I am perfect the way I am. I would not change a thing. I am unique, and my life experiences have brought me to this moment in time. My story is not finished with a lifetime of adventures ahead of me. I am excited and thankful that I am truly present in my life.

Living and Journaling Using Your Values For Self-Discovery

Journaling Through Conversation 3

Experience what it feels like to live in line with my values.

How can my values support me to develop more awareness about myself while caregiving on my self-discovery path?

The following worksheet will help you articulate and understand your values to support you in becoming more self-aware. You will learn to consciously use these core values as guides through your daily life by paying attention to how you feel while experiencing living in line with them, as well as when you feel misaligned with them. Through daily journaling, you will discover what is most important to you to live with more self-awareness.

Things to Consider Regarding Bringing Your Values into Your Daily Decision-Making:

- Find self-awareness within your values;
- Know what your values are;
- Bring them out when you are making decisions;
- Be aware of the emotional feelings you experience when living in line with your values;
- Your values and how you can articulate them within experiences will help you navigate situations;
- Use the Arc of Intense Energy for support if you are unsure about how to move forward towards showing up in line with your values as your authentic self.

Find self-awareness within your values:

Have you ever found yourself asking these questions *Who am I? What is next? Where do I go from here?* while you are caregiving and experiencing many demands within your life? There comes a time when awareness and desire are needed to move forward and experience life with more joy, understanding, and purpose.

Awareness is the first step to finding your way beyond grief and uncertainty, the need to answer the questions mentioned above. It is the beginning of the curiosity and ability to face fear and the unknown with courage while searching for answers. While caregiving, there will be a time when you will no longer have to support your loved one. At this time, you can choose to begin the journey to find yourself. You may explore more authentically and true to your inner voice.

My hope is that, as a caregiver, the process of living more authentically with a deeper understanding of your values will help you create foundational daily practices that help you grow within your inner-self and support you to manage the demands of a caregiver.

You may ask, *How can I do this?* The first steps are to quiet your mind and slow down. Your daily life and demands on your time are overwhelming. You are on autopilot. You can start to journal to get your thoughts and emotions on paper, sit and listen to music, read self-help or spiritual books, take up running or yoga, paint, or engage in other creative activities. Choose an activity that allows you to reconnect with your inner self, the part of you that is your true authentic self - the voice within you -rather than the part you may be showing the world.

As you start this journey, you may find yourself wanting to know more and being open to change and letting go of the past. This could be after your caregiving role has ended or while you are currently within this role. There is a grieving process needed to let go of the beliefs and patterns you have carried with you most of your life. You might be realizing that the thoughts and patterns you experience in your everyday life are not necessarily correct or true. You may have believed from a young age that you didn't have a voice. An event or someone may have sent you a message that you are to be seen and not heard, creating a belief that you have nothing to say.

When you discover your values and understand what is important for your well-being, you can challenge these thoughts and determine what is true and what is not. When you are not living in line with your values, you may experience fear, sadness, anxiety, confusion, doubt, or defeat - the uncomfortable feelings. When living in line with your values, you will strengthen positive feelings like joy, bliss, connectedness, and confidence.

Know what values are:

Values are deeply held beliefs about what is important to you. Essentially, they are your *bottom line*. Learn what your values are so you can write them down and bring them into your daily awareness. Understand the emotion you experience while living in line with each of your values. As you progress through life and become more familiar with your values, they may change their order and importance depending on where you are on your life's path.

Be mindful of the emotional feelings you experience when living in line with your values:

There may be times when you encounter situations that require choice and action that isn't always easy. And there will be times of opportunity that require difficult choice as well. Some include:

- Seeing someone behave in a way that you feel is unethical;
- Being reminded of an uncomfortable memory through an experience or interaction;
- Being approached by someone in a way you are not comfortable with;
- Being put in a situation that creates a conflict of interest;
- Behaving in a way that isn't congruent with your values when under stress. You may react in a way you wish you hadn't and not realize it until after you did it;
- Being faced with an incredible opportunity and needing to make a decision that could change your life.

Know what your values are:

Spend some time articulating your values and keep them with you. Share your values and have a conversation about them with others. This helps to deepen your understanding and commitment to them. Check them against other possible values to understand trade-offs and ensure these are the most important ones for you. Use the values exercise on the next page to articulate yours and list them in the chart on the following page.

Your values and how you articulate them will support you to navigate situations. Take the time to discover your top 8 core values. You may have many values, so place a checkmark beside the values words that resonate with you in the list below, and then choose just 8 to use throughout this workbook:

Values Words - Common Personal Values[4]

Accomplishment,
Success
Accountability
Accuracy
Adventure
Beauty
Calm, quietude, peace
Challenge
Change
Cleanliness, orderliness
Collaboration
Commitment
Communication
Community
Competence
Competition
Concern for others
Content over form
Continuous improvement
Cooperation
Coordination
Creativity
Decisiveness
Delight of being, joy
Discipline
Discovery
Ease of Use
Efficiency
Equality
Excellence
Fairness
Faith
Family

Family feeling
Freedom
Friendship
Fun
Good will
Goodness
Gratitude
Hard work
Harmony
Health & Wellness
Honesty
Honor
Independence
Inner peace, calm, quietude
Innovation
Integrity
Justice
Knowledge
Leadership
Love, Romance
Loyalty
Meaning
Merit
Money
Openness
Peace, Non-violence
Perfection
Personal Growth
Pleasure
Positive attitude
Power
Practicality
Preservation

Privacy
Problem Solving
Progress
Prosperity, Wealth
Punctuality
Quality of work
Regularity Resourcefulness
Respect for others
Responsiveness
Results-oriented
Safety
Satisfying others
Security
Self-discovery
Self-reliance
Simplicity
Skill
Spirit in life
Spirituality
Stability
Status
Strength
Teamwork
Tolerance
Tradition
Tranquility
Trust
Truth
Unity
Variety
Wisdom

---

[4] From the Internet – Original Source no longer available.

You may have checked off many or just a few. Either way, narrow them down to 8 values you feel strongly about and write them in the chart below:

	My Top 8 Core Values:
1	
2	
3	
4	
5	
6	
7	
8	

Values' Feelings:

Now, let's customize your values and make them uniquely yours by connecting them to the feelings or emotions you experience when living in line with them:

We all have similar values that are a natural expression of living, such as *work, community service, family and relationships*. The difference is that the importance of each of our values will change over time, depending where you are on your life's path. The value may not change, but the focus and priority in which you place your value will change. For example, in your twenties, the values you focus on may be work, finances, family and friends, and wellness; in that order. But, in your thirties, these values may shift in priority as you may be raising a family. Your values are unique to your life. This exercise will support you to articulate your values in order of what is currently important to you, while understanding the emotions associated with them and your experiences. For example, *When I'm living in line with my work value, the feeling I experience is efficiency. I feel productive and satisfied as I work through my daily tasks productively and with ease. There is a flow within my work that allows time to slip away, and before I know it, my workday is done. When I am not living in line with my value of work, I feel inefficient. This is felt within my body as the emotional feelings of anxiety and discomfort as I am not feeling productive within my workday. I feel that I can't stay on task because I am easily distracted and unable to get into the flow of my work.*

For Example:

My Values	Emotional Feeling
Work	Efficiency

Another example, *When I reflect on my value of Community Service, if all is aligned, the emotion I feel is meaningful. When I am true to myself within my service to others, whether it be volunteering, helping clients on their path to self-discovery, or supporting individuals in my community, I am aware of how in line I am with my Community Service value because I feel meaningful when supporting others. When I am in a similar situation but feeling overwhelmed because I am in a larger group and unable to connect on a more personal level, I feel unimportant because I connect on a deeper level in a one-on-one situation. During these times I feel I am not making a difference in the lives of those I am of service to. Journaling allows me to become more aware of when I feel insignificant and allows me to re-evaluate what I am experiencing within my value of Community Service to make changes that provide me with feeling more meaningful. The conclusion is that I need to make a change by serving others in smaller groups or one-on-one.*

For Example:

My Values	Emotional Feeling
Community Service	Meaningful

The emotional feeling experienced within each personal value is much more significant than the title of the value it represents. You are becoming more aware of your emotions and how they resonate within your soul to guide you, especially experiencing the *Arc* from Conversation 1. What is helpful is the awareness of when you feel the opposite of the emotion you resonate with, the uncomfortable emotional response. You can choose to slow down and provide yourself with the space of time and energy to shift to a way of being that reflects your values and the feelings you pick to represent them. You can take the opportunity to journal during these indecisive times to articulate your feelings in writing and discover how they feel within your body as well. While in your caregiving role, you may feel invisible at times because the focus is on your loved one while navigating their health care and emotional needs. This is when it is important to know your values in order to stay connected with your inner voice.

Using each of your values and their feelings will support you to manage the Arc of Intense Energy, guiding you towards showing up as your authentic self:

This brings us back to the Arc of Intense Energy because when we enter the *Arc* due to a trigger we experience, we feel the opposite feeling of one or more of our top core values. Some describe them as negative feelings, and we often ignore them or subconsciously block them because they are difficult to experience – they may bring up memories of trauma from our past that we would rather not think about. When a feeling or emotion like this arises, it is our soul's way of asking us to pay attention and be curious about what we are feeling. Now is the time to step back and reflect on what we are feeling; what value(s) are being compromised in that moment? How do you want to respond in a way that is authentic to you? You have the choice to slow down and find clarity about what is arising in you and why. When you take that time and those few breaths in response to the discomfort, you provide yourself with the choice to determine how you want to proceed and respond in a way that feels right for you and in line with your values. This is how to use your values and the feelings associated with them as guideposts towards living in a more self-aware way.

For example: My value of Community Service and the emotional feeling of Connection through caregiving:

A significant piece of my Community Service Value is using my self-discovery path through grief, loss, trauma, and caregiver burnout to connect with those experiencing the same and share my knowledge and ability to listen and understand exactly where they are at this time. There is a sense of calm, knowing I can provide the space of empathy and understanding for what someone may be experiencing and feeling. I find comfort knowing I can unlock how I feel within the conversations I have with my soul through my daily journaling practice.

Exercise gives me the same feeling of connection, whether I am walking or running, cycling or swimming. It provides me with the same experience as it allows my mind to wander and connect to what I believe and feel deeply. So, when I experience a lack of connection, I know I need to choose one of these practices to guide me back to feeling connected again. I always go to journaling first to release my thoughts on paper; exercise is next. Inspired thoughts come freely when I am walking in nature or exercising because I am present within the activity and feel connected to my inner voice – my soul.

Understanding and being aware of your emotional feelings can provide new awareness within your decision-making as you ask yourself questions during moments of journaling when emotions arise.

As your journaling practice evolves and you become more comfortable with it, you will begin to feel and understand the power of connecting with your inner voice – your soul. Journaling will reveal more understanding about your values, who you are, and where you are heading on your path of self-discovery through the process of caregiving.

Arc of Intense Energy Reflection:

Refer to the diagram and description of the Arc of Intense Energy in Conversation 1. Reflect on the topic of this chapter – *Living and Journaling Using Your Values For Self-Discovery*. Answer the following questions to understand how the Arc is showing up for you:

What is your old, automatic pattern when triggered? For example, *My old pattern would be to ignore my inner voice letting me know that I needed to listen to my own needs. I would not feel motivated too uncomfortable writing what I am feeling:*

What is a new behaviour, belief or attitude you would like to choose instead? For example, *I know that as I journal and work through the emotions and patterns of my past, I am creating a new authentic way of being, which will bring more joy and purpose into my life:*

Practice self-managing through the *Arc* when you are learning about living true to your values. Begin by paying attention, noticing the energy or discomfort intensifying in the body. As this occurs, practice relaxing your shoulders and belly and deepen and slow your breathing.
This will allow you to feel the emotions as they arise, notice your thoughts and determine if they are aligned with your values or just old, unhelpful messages. Write about these emotions and thoughts in your journal.

When you learn to understand what is true and right, you will be able to articulate and understand how to respond to uncomfortable situations in life. While caregiving, you will feel intense emotions, but you will be able to determine where they are coming from and make decisions that serve both you and your loved one. For example, your Arc may be presenting from a place of personal fatigue or frustration within a caregiving situation.

By managing your response to the *Arc* through journaling, you will be able to find a new self-awareness about what to do next while shifting old patterns and thoughts.

Action Steps

Exercise:

Use the values you articulated above and add corresponding feelings to the value's titles you come up with. These feelings are translated from your values through this process, and you will use them to guide you through difficult times and decisions, as well as through your journaling to reveal your true inner voice – your soul - and the truth within you.

My Values	**Emotional Feeling**

Reflections:

- Reflecting on your values, what are you learning about yourself? How are your values showing up in your daily journaling practice? Use meditation to support this process while calming your nervous system and finding a place where you feel grounded:

- What common thread is your journaling presenting? What do you need to do to inspire a more authentic way of being?

- What value do you find you are misaligned with if you don't spend time journaling to reflect on the emotions and challenges within your caregiving day? What one thing can you do to show up more in line with that value?

Practice taking action to live in ways that are in line with your values and the feelings that correspond with them; see how these actions present within your journaling:

When you begin working with your values, you learn to create a different way of thinking about your life. Imagine re-hardwiring your brain with a new way that may feel uncomfortable if your automatic pattern, like many others, is to live in ways that are not in line with your values. Give yourself a chance. Remember, it will take time and having compassion for yourself will support you as you begin these practices.

- Write down a current situation where you live in a way that is in line with your values :

- How do you know? What is the feeling or emotion you feel when you live aligned with who you are and what is important to you? For example, *I feel joy and at peace:*

- Write down a current situation where you live in a way that is not in line with your values:

- Again, how do you know? What does it feel like when you are out of alignment with your values? For example, *I feel depressed, and there is a hollow feeling in my chest:*

- What can you do differently in your life to live more fully aligned with your values?

Understanding and living in line with your values and trusting how you feel can provide you with internal guidance to support you at times of uncertainty and not knowing the next step going forward. As you become more aware of your values, you will be able to create boundaries in a situation to help you navigate life more authentically.

Continued Daily Practices to Support Discovering Your Values Through Journaling:

Review the foundational practices you have been committing to. If you feel comfortable with all of them, continue including them in your daily routine. However, if you are not resonating with one or more, or if you are trying to do too many, take the time to discover which ones and the pace you prefer practicing to create a mindset that promotes physical, emotional, and spiritual presence.

Stick with the free-flow activities you have been enjoying. If you have too much space, feel free to add a different activity or switch any out for another like listening to music.

What's Next? Have a Conversation With Your Soul Through Journaling:

What is your soul saying to you about your values? How are you feeling about using them as guides through your role as a caregiver, and how can you express this through journaling – having a conversation with your soul? Grab your journal and write what you are discovering about yourself.

A Conversation With My Soul
By Donna Fitzgerald

Who am I?

Who am I? Where did I Go?
Have you seen Donna? Where did she go?
I wake up and look in the mirror in search of the woman I knew, and yet, I go to bed feeling isolated, exhausted, and empty.

How did I get here?

I am married to a wonderful man and have two children who I love beyond words. Something else moved into my life, and I was not prepared for its insistence on taking over my family. It was ALS. At first, I accepted the disease as something I would face with my husband, and we would get through it on our terms. Little did I know that was not to be my reality as I was in for the fight of my life with the monster called ALS.

I woke up every day with the sole purpose of loving my family and caring for their needs, trying to make life as normal as it could be with home care, mobility devices, and fear of what was ahead.

I would go off to work every day, hoping that everything did not fall apart while I was away from my family and that my children did not feel neglected and alone. Before I knew it, four years of caregiving had passed, and I had so many more new roles in life that I was not prepared for. I watched my husband fight every day to stay in our lives. My reality was that I had hit my breaking point, and I could no longer care for him at home.

I realized that there was one person I forgot to love and put on the list - that was myself. I was so busy caring for everyone else that I forgot Donna. I thought it was selfish to think of my needs, and people would judge me if I wasn't caring for my family. I was so wrong!

I found myself alone with my thoughts and terrified that I had lost who I was. I knew my roles in life, but I no longer knew myself. I understood my husband would die from ALS, and my children would lose their father to this disease. I also realized I had given all of me to ALS.

This day of awareness sparked the need to change my life - to fight to find myself and not let ALS take me down. I needed to be strong within who I am to continue to support and love my husband for all his life and raise my children.

The key to finding myself began by being still, learning to take time to quiet my mind and start listening to my body by journaling the emotions and thoughts I had pushed down for a lifetime. This is not an easy task when you are afraid of what may be revealed. If I open the door, will the anger, frustration, and tears overwhelm me and open a flood gate that I can't close? I had no choice but to start taking care of myself - exercise, nutrition, sleep, and fun.

I had to fit these into my chaotic day. If I managed to make one small change, it was a start. There was no looking back. I was determined to take this journey of self-discovery.

In time, I began to feel stronger, and I became more prepared to face my day and the death of my husband. I had to learn to let go of the past and the thought of how my life should look. I had today, and I would face every day at the moment and try not to feel guilt for not doing everything perfectly or the way others thought I should.

It has been ten years since I experienced the feeling of losing myself. I have the memories of a wonderful husband who taught me to live life with humour, determination, and integrity. I have raised two young adults who fill my heart with love every day.

The most amazing gift has been that in loving myself, I have found I have grown to love who I am and accept all *of me. I have learned to keep my memories of the past in my heart and live today as if there is no tomorrow. I know tomorrow will come, and life has its challenges, but I am a survivor, and I am blessed with one more day. I not only found Donna; I love the woman I have become.*

Using Your Inner Purpose Feeling To Connect With Your Soul

Journaling Through Conversation 4

Experience what it feels like to use your Inner Purpose Feeling through self-discovery.

How can being aware of your Inner Purpose Feeling support you to connect with your soul within the journey of caregiving?

TThe following worksheet will guide you to identify your Inner Purpose Feeling.[5]
It is the emotional feeling you experience when living in line with your values.
This will support you to move through self-discovery while caregiving.
Use your journaling and Inner Purpose Feeling to support making changes in your life
aligned with your authentic Self.

Things to Consider When Using Your Inner Purpose Feeling To Connect With Your Soul:

- Your Inner Purpose Feeling (IPF) is how you feel when you are living and experiencing life in line with all your values;
- Your Inner Purpose Feeling 3-step process can be used as a guide for decision-making when responding to people and experiences when caring for your loved one;
- Re-consider your decisions if you discover the emotion you are experiencing is uncomfortable and not aligned with your Inner Purpose Feeling – when experiencing the Arc of Intense Energy;
- When unsure, make the space to step back and tune into how you are feeling emotionally;
- Your Inner Purpose Feeling and the Arc of Intense Energy are authentic tools that work together to support you within the journaling process as you navigate your role as a caregiver.

---

[5] Inner Purpose Feeling: Diana Reyers, Founder of Daring to Share Global

Inner Purpose Feeling (IPF):

In Conversation 3, you discovered your values and the emotional feelings associated with each of them in order to make choices in line with them when you feel stuck – when you are on the Arc of Intense Energy. The Inner Purpose Feeling is the emotional feeling you resonate with and experience when choosing to live in line with all your values at the same time, true to your authentic self. It validates your beliefs and supports you to do, say, and be what is right for you within your caregiving role.

Your Inner Purpose Feeling is how you feel when you are living and experiencing life in line with all your values:

When you choose to fully feel, both physically and emotionally, you give yourself the ability to be present and curious about why you feel the way you do. To give you more ease, it can help to narrow down your values' feelings to one that resonates with you. This is your Inner Purpose Feeling. It is the one emotion created when you are living in line with all your values at the same time. This is what it would feel like if you were living as your authentic or best-self a lot of the time, including while caring for your loved one. How amazing would that be?!

The Inner Purpose Feeling 3-step process can be used as a guide for decision-making when responding to people and experiences and when caring for a loved one:

1. Be mindful of your inner voice, when your soul speaks to you, and the emotion you feel within a particular situation or interaction with someone – comfortable or uncomfortable;
2. Take a moment to slow down to listen to what your inner voice is saying to you and the emotional feeling you are experiencing; determine what value(s) and your established associated emotional feeling(s) may be compromised within your behaviour, what you are saying, or what you are thinking, or the same of someone in your presence – review your values and your associated emotional feelings in Conversation 3;
3. Use your Inner Purpose Feeling to find clarity about how you want to respond, in line with your values, to this particular experience, situation, or person.

In order to do this, you need to discover and articulate one overarching emotion – one word – that encompasses how you feel when experiencing all your values' emotional feelings at once. To narrow it down to just one, take the time to experience each value's emotion and discover a common feeling that is created when living in line with them. When you live in line with all of your values' feelings at the same time within a situation or while interacting with someone, you will experience one cumulative emotional feeling. For example, When I use my values' feelings of strength, love, truth, meaning, and efficiency to guide me through difficult times, the cumulative emotional feeling I experience is Calm.

Re-consider your decisions if you discover the emotion you are experiencing is uncomfortable and not aligned with your Inner Purpose Feeling – when experiencing the Arc of Intense Energy:

Once you have clarity about what this one expansive feeling is, you will have a deep knowing when you don't feel it or when you feel uncomfortable emotions. You can then make changes within the situation and your way of being to move towards your Inner Purpose Feeling by choosing how you respond to situations and people and anything that may come up within your daily caregiving. This, in turn, provides you with clarity about how you want to show up in the world. You will be confident and decisive and able to live each day a little more fully with more self-awareness about what you want to do, be, and say. This will support you towards a more authentic way of being.

For example, my Inner Purpose Feeling is Calm, and my Enneagram personality is the Peacemaker, and I want to help everyone. When I feel balanced within my everyday life, I feel a sense of calm; when I don't, I feel anxious within every aspect of my being, life, and supportive role. When I was a caregiver for my husband for six years, working full-time, raising our family, providing emotional support and nursing care to my husband, I tried to keep our home life as normal as possible. I forgot that I, too, needed to be on the list of care. Overtime, while trying to keep everyone happy, healthy and maintain my standard of productivity at work, I realized I could not keep up this pace. As I was looking after everyone else, I was losing myself. I finally hit my breaking point when my body and emotions said, *You can no longer do this; changes have to be made* - I realized I had lost myself, I did not know what made me happy or who I was.

I only knew my roles in life. It was terrifying. After making changes to my daily routines and making needed changes to my husband's care, I started to regain myself in time. Over several years I worked through the process of rediscovering myself and using the tool of journaling to connect with my inner voice, my soul. I am now living in line with my inner purpose of Calm more of the time. I still have challenges within my life, and I still love to support all those in my life and community. The difference is that I now have boundaries around what I can and cannot do. I know how to redirect my life when I feel that I am moving away from my sense of Calm. I start with my journaling, which creates the space for me to evaluate where the unbalance is and what changes I need to make to move me back into my Inner Purpose Feeling.

When unsure, make the space to step back and tune into how you are feeling emotionally:

Life will always present challenges and moments when you choose to ignore your Inner Purpose Feeling. When this happens, you will experience uncomfortable emotional feelings, and in turn, this provides you with the choice to slow down and learn even more about yourself. When you take the time to understand your emotions during challenging times, you create the opportunity to assess why you are experiencing them and discover how to move through them more quickly.

It is important to experience these challenges and have clarity about your emotional feelings in order to understand yourself better. With each situation, you can learn how to adjust your approach the next time, so you respond in line with your values by using your IPF as a guide.

When I find myself in a situation that I am unsure how to navigate, I focus on my daily wellness practices to gain clarity and understand what my inner-self needs. I sit in meditation and then journal and let my emotions and thoughts reveal themselves. I then have a better understanding of why I feel a certain way and can focus on gaining information or the support I need to move back to a state of being that is in line with my Inner Purpose Feeling of Calm. Sometimes, it is difficult to face the parts that contribute to how I feel and that I would like to keep hidden. As I move through the lesson or life experience, I grow and gain confidence and compassion for myself. I am living life more authentically and show up in the world around me living my truth, even when that truth is not always comfortable.

Your Inner Purpose Feeling and the Arc of Intense Energy are authentic tools that work together to support you within the journaling process as you navigate your role as a caregiver:

The Arc of Intense Energy allows you to experience when you are out of alignment with your Inner Purpose Feeling – your values – right away, more of the time. You will feel the discomfort of the misalignment in your body with a physical sensation first and then within how you feel emotionally.

With practice, you will eventually know when you are out of alignment very quickly. It is your physical body that sends you the first red flag. It is a physical response telling you there is something compromising your Inner Purpose Feeling, your values. You may get a flip in your stomach, or the hair on the back of your neck may stand up as you begin to overthink within an awareness of a presented trigger. This is your soul sending you a message that you need to become aware of what is happening and understand why it doesn't feel right for you – you are experiencing the opposite physical sensation that supports your Inner Purpose Feeling. Your intuition wants you to discover why, so you can correct your course.

If you choose to ignore your physical response, you will move further up the *Arc* and feel the uncomfortable emotion that aligns with it. You may feel angry, nervous, anxious, fearful or ashamed among some; all the uncomfortable emotional feelings that are the opposite of your values' feelings and your IPF. This is your soul, giving you another chance as it begs you to become aware of what you need in order to show up in line with your authentic self. It's time to pay attention so you can shift and choose to respond in your truth, in line with your IPF.

Arc of Intense Energy Writing Reflection:

Refer to the diagram and description of the Arc of Intense Energy in Conversation 1. Reflect on the topic of this Conversation – *Using Your Inner Purpose Feeling To Connect With Your Soul*. Answer the following questions in order to understand how the *Arc* is showing up for you:

What is your old, automatic pattern when triggered? Where is your inner critical voice triggering you? For example, *My old, automatic pattern is to retreat and shut down, to hide. The little girl within me comes out with my pattern of "you are to be seen and not heard." I have no voice. This is how I showed up in life before caregiving. As I started to create a new life of self-awareness, I realized I did have a voice; I was to be heard:*

What is a new behaviour, belief or attitude you would like to choose instead? For example: *Through my daily journaling practice, I have learned to have a conversation with my soul. To understand myself from a deeper place within myself. I now choose to speak my truth as it is revealed through my words:*

Practice self-managing through the Arc when you are moving through your day and while in your caregiving role or when spending time alone. Begin by paying attention, noticing the energy or discomfort intensifying in the body. As this occurs, practice relaxing your shoulders and belly and deepen and slow your breathing. Realize this too shall pass.

This will allow you to feel the emotions as they arise, notice your thoughts and determine if they are aligned with your values or if they are just old, unhelpful messages.

When you discover which is true and right, you will be able to maintain your perspective and choose an appropriate and authentic response for the situation at hand. And, you will become decisive in the way you choose to live…for now.

After a few weeks of practicing, reflect on what you are learning and how you will adjust your thoughts and behaviours as a result.

Action Steps

Reflections:

Use the values and corresponding emotional feelings you articulated in Conversation 3 to reflect on and discover how you would describe the one emotion you experience when responding to people and situations in line with all your values' feelings simultaneously. This is an opportunity to use journaling to support you to find clarity about how you want to feel most of the time:

Exercise:

Define your Inner Purpose Feeling to further clarify how you want to feel most of the time. Use your IPF as an articulation of your combined values' feelings and allow it to guide you through indecisiveness and uncomfortable moments:

For Example:

My Values	Emotional Feelings Associated with My Values	Inner Purpose Feeling (One Emotion)
Well-Being	Commitment	Calm
Relationship	Love	
Community Service	Meaning	
Spirituality	Truth	
Work	Efficiency	

Write down your values and their corresponding feelings. Then, with one word, describe the overarching emotion you feel when living in line with all your values at the same time. This is your IPF – keep it top of your mind as you journal.

My Values	Emotional Feelings Associated with My Values	Inner Purpose Feeling (One Emotion)

Your Inner Purpose Feeling is an authentic tool to use while journaling as you navigate the process of caregiving:

Your Inner Purpose Feeling will support you as you move forward on your path to self-discovery. It will provide you with the ability to tune into how you feel when you are living authentically, resonating with your IPF, and how you feel when you are not. These are cues from your soul, asking you to slow down and listen so you have the capacity to choose to journal and reveal the truth that lies within you – to live more in line with your authentic self, most of the time. When you feel stuck and not in line with your IPF, ask yourself the following questions:

- What am I feeling right now? For example, *I remember a time while caregiving when I felt anxious on my way home from work. I could feel the emotion intensifying as I drove closer to home:*

- What is causing me to feel this? For example, *Growing more anxious, I asked myself why I was feeling this way. I realized that I was not sure what mood my husband would be in when I arrived home. During this time of his disease, he was angry and his only way to express himself was by wanting me to be available to him at all times. If I wasn't, he would lash out verbally or physically by running into me with his wheelchair:*

- What am I journaling that is not aligned with my Inner Purpose Feeling? For example, *Through my journaling, I realized that my family was in crisis and out of alignment with the feeling of calm. We were all exhausted and in need of respite. My children and I had found spaces within our home where we would retreat to when we felt overwhelmed. Through my journaling, I knew it was time for a conversation with my husband's physician regarding his care and keeping our family safe:*

- What is causing me to feel the opposite of my Inner Purpose Feeling? For example, *I am making decisions related to the challenges I am experiencing in my caregiving that are not in line with my values. Or, I am ignoring what needs to be acknowledged because I know I will need to respond in a different way:*

- How can my journaling help me to process the emotions that are uncomfortable and that may be opening old wounds or past experiences? For example, *I discovered through my writing that committing to the next steps I needed to take for my family's safety meant opening up emotions of abandonment that I felt as a child. I also knew that my husband would view my need for respite as abandonment as well. This was not the case; we had just hit another stage and roadblock within the progression of his disease and my ability to provide safe care:*

Using your Inner Purpose Feeling is your guide to leading a more authentic life and journaling authentically. It is the next step towards really stepping into your truth and practicing the fundamentals of the Arc of Intense Energy. The more you practice managing the *Arc*, the more confidence you will achieve as you feel morally and ethically aligned with your values and with doing the right thing for you and others within your daily living and through your journaling process.

Continued Daily Practices to Support Determining Your Inner Purpose Feeling Through Journaling:

Review the foundational practices you have been committing to. If you feel comfortable with all of them, continue including them in your daily routine. However, if you are not resonating with one or more, take the time to discover what you prefer practicing to create a mindset that promotes physical, emotional, and spiritual presence.

Stick with the free-flow activities you have been enjoying. If you have space, feel free to add a different activity or switch any out for another like cooking or baking something special. If you have too much going on, let go of one to make space for rest.

What's Next? Have a Conversation With Your Soul Through Journaling:

What is your soul saying to you about what your Inner Purpose Feeling is? What emotion are you using to describe how you would like to feel most of the time, and how can you express this through journaling – having a conversation with your soul? Grab your journal and write what you are discovering about yourself.

A Conversation With My Soul
By Donna Fitzgerald

Learning to Trust Myself

As I moved forward from the grief of loss, I began to listen to my inner voice to trust my gut feeling and push through the fear. Life doesn't come with a manual, and if it did, I was sure I was missing a few chapters.

I started journaling and getting my thoughts on paper daily. I could clear my mind by journaling my questions were sometimes revealed unexpectedly.

I started to meditate. I remember the first time I tried meditation at my workplace. There was a meditation group that met at lunchtime a couple of days a week. I thought maybe this was what I needed to help cope with the stress of my life.

I tried several times over a few weeks. I would sit quietly and start to meditate, but my body must have thought it was time to sleep; I would start to fall asleep and felt worse after 20 minutes. I was sleep-deprived, not having slept through the night in over two years with my caregiver routine in the evening - tube feedings and repositioning my husband, My body just wanted to shut down if given the opportunity.

In time, my life settled down after the death of my husband. I thought, ok it is time to try meditation again. It was hard to sit still, and I physically wanted to get up or move positions. My mind would dash about with thoughts of laundry to do, grocery lists, activities of the day. It is not easy to clear your mind. I had been living in overdrive for so long it was difficult to be still.

I started to listen to my breath and concentrate on breathing in and breathing out; I would tell myself to push the thoughts out of my head. I am still learning how to meditate but feel so relaxed and centred when I take the time to just be.

I realized through journaling and meditation that I was much more than my thoughts. I had grown up thinking I was ugly, insecure, shy and invisible. I was becoming more aware of why and what experiences as a child had formed these thought patterns. By facing my past, I had a new view of me. Now I realize the view of me is shaped by fear and insecurities rooted in my childhood abuse.

I started communicating more loving thoughts to myself; you are smart, kind, beautiful, compassionate and loving - all words I had not heard before. I started to believe in myself and understand that I didn't have to please anyone but myself. I am learning to be true to who I am and be myself.

As I started to trust in myself and gain confidence within myself, my world has opened. I don't want to just exist within my life. I want to live life and experience it. I still experience fear in times of change and uncertainty, but I now can determine whether the fear is attached to old

thoughts; this is a reminder to use my new daily practice to sit and feel the fear and journal to ask the questions. Why do I feel this way? Will I hurt myself if I try this new experience? If I push through the fear, what exciting new experience is on the other side?

I now know that the only one keeping me stuck is myself. I am the only one with myself until the day I die, so I am determined to be the best I can be. I will keep learning about myself and what I am capable of. The world is mine; all I need to do is take a deep breath and a leap of faith and jump in.

Discovering More About Yourself By Managing Your Inner Critic

Journaling Through Conversation 5

Understanding your inner critic messages.

How can you use your inner critic to determine what you believe and feel while caregiving and discovering more about yourself?

The following worksheet will assist you in becoming more aware of the inner critic as it relates to living your authentic life. It will also support you to take the first steps to begin to live and journal with more freedom from your inner critic.

Things to Consider About Discovering More About Yourself By Managing Your Inner Critic:

- The inner critic will always be there, and as you become aware of it, it may become even louder;
- It is possible to shift how you experience the inner critic when it comes up and then reduce its impact on your life;
- Compassion is the gateway both for others and for yourself;
- The Arc of Intense Energy is an effective tool supporting you to recognize and manage the inner critic;
- Judgments can be created through projections.

The inner critic will always be there, and as you become aware of it, it may become even louder:

What is the inner critic? When, Where, and How does it show up in your life?

Spending time over the past twenty years on my path of self-discovery, I realize that my inner critic was developed when I was a young girl. I can now articulate and understand that my inner critic kept me silent and afraid. I was sexually abused by my father when I was a young girl. My inner critic kept me silent - *don't tell your secret, remain invisible. No one can know.* I became the shy, introverted girl that always did what she was told. If I was good, no one would question me or my behaviour. I learned how to please the people in my life and keep everyone happy;

In my teens, I was a target and bullied in high school. I was shy and felt ugly with low self-esteem. I was afraid of boys, and they sensed they could tease me, and they did. I liked school for the learning aspect but never felt like I fit in socially. When I was thirteen, I broke my dresser's mirror with my fist; I felt ugly and invisible. As time went on, all I wanted was to be a wife and mother. Would I be able to find someone to love me? In my early twenties, I met my husband, and we connected with similar traumatic childhoods - my abuse as a child and his being raised by two alcoholic parents. He left high school early to work because he could no longer be at home with the alcohol and the fights within his home. We were both looking for a way out of our family situations. We were both looking to raise our family in a very different environment, and we understood each other's past.

It wasn't until my husband was diagnosed with ALS, and I was experiencing caregiver burnout and the loss of self in my mid-forties that I realized how my childhood had shaped me as an adult. As I started to commit to healing from my trauma, grief, burnout and loss of self, I began to realize that I was not living authentically to who I was deep within my soul. My husband was my best friend, and we loved each other deeply. I am grateful every day for his love and his gift of strength through his illness, allowing me to do the personal work as I continue to uncover the untruths of my past.

Through journaling, I learned to understand my inner critic by asking myself questions about the thoughts and emotional feelings I experience. For example, *Why am I feeling insignificant and invisible and not speaking up?*

This provided me with the option to continuously manage my inner critic by finding clarity about the questions I have about how I feel.

It is possible to shift how you experience the inner critic when it comes up and then reduce its impact on your life:

As I discovered more about my inner critic and became familiar with its messages to me, I was able to ask myself questions to unravel what was true through the learned behaviours of my childhood. My journaling served a vital role in unloading emotional feelings that I locked away my whole life. Through writing and every new thought, awareness, and untrue pattern I revealed, I became more confident and open to knowing more about myself. I have experienced a new knowing of my inner voice and soul.

I can determine when my inner critic is speaking from a past pattern or thought, and I have become more authentic and in tune with my inner voice - my soul. My inner critic has become a welcomed part of my being. I now have the confidence to really evaluate my thoughts and connect with my values and Inner Purpose Feeling and receive the true message my inner critic is telling me. Maybe it is something I still need to heal, or maybe it is just a warning to be careful, or maybe it is merely a thought I can let go.

I now realize that as a child, my inner critic's voice was my father, always chiming in, *You need to be silent, invisible and be a good girl*. Now I understand that, in some ways, my inner critic saved me from being a rebel and lashing out through addictive behaviours that would not have served me well. As a woman, wife, and mother, my inner critic silently created this expectation that I had to take care of my family perfectly at the expense of my losing myself.

Compassion is the gateway both for yourself and others.
Managing the inner critic by using compassion for yourself:

One way the inner critic presents itself is when one or more of our values is being compromised, either by how we choose to show up, how someone else is showing up, or within an experience we may be struggling with. Remember, it's a thought that just lasts a few seconds, but can stay longer if we focus on it and allow it to replay over and over in our mind:

- In its basic form, the inner critic is the internalization of the messages we received as children and young adults from society and others who influenced us at that time;
- It can then extend into an interpretation we create from something someone said or did without understanding what their intention was;
- The inner critic is often developed within a culture we live in, a religion we are guided by, or the society we are surrounded by;
- If we allow ourselves to manage and befriend it, we can learn to step into our full power more of the time and despite it;
- It can be managed by seeing it, understanding where it came from, keeping it in perspective, laughing at it at times, screaming at it inside our heads sometimes, and practicing placing a boundary around it and then letting it go;
- Its volume can get louder or softer at times depending on our capacity based on our level of well-being and whether or not we have our foundational practices in place;

- There are very few who do not have an inner critic, and some sense it as a feeling, emotional or somatic, or both, rather than hear it as a voice. When we are very aware, we are able to feel it somatically -physically - when it first approaches, and then as an emotional feeling shortly after;
- Your inner critic enters as a somatic feeling when you begin approaching the Arc of Intense Energy. It is sneaky and may be mean, so you need to be mindful in order to feel it in your body; step back, listen to what it says, find clarity, and then choose to agree or not;
- Practicing self-compassion is very helpful as you build the ability to create boundaries around what you will allow her to be a part of, and what you won't by using your values and your Inner Purpose Feeling as guideposts; is what she is saying in line with my values, or not? The answer to this question creates clarity and validation;
- Practicing compassion within your caregiving role will support you to understand that it is not selfish to recognize the need for your self-care. This will provide you with the strength and endurance you need to support your loved one as long as it is required;
- A community of support is helpful when you find it difficult to decide or manage your inner critic in certain situations and when feeling controlled by her.

Managing the inner critic by using compassion and empathy for others:

When I sense a strong inner critic in someone, it is usually a result of them experiencing self-talk during our conversations. The example I experience the most is when someone is given a compliment and immediately responds in a way that diminishes its intent. The way I experienced this was when I felt invisible and not feel worthy of another's praise.

Are you able to accept positive feedback? Are you able to really take it in and feel it? What about negative feedback? The positive to negative ratio needs to be 5:1 in order to balance the impact of the negative and hear the positive. It's much easier to see the negative, and it takes effort and practice to choose a balanced perspective in the moment. Being mindful can provide the opportunity to achieve this:

- Negative self-talk can be an indication of how judgmental we are of ourselves, which can then show up in the way we treat others;
- This may involve projections - what we believe, we sense in someone else, or project onto them, which then arises as judgment towards others. It may be a projection on them of something that would be too painful to see in ourselves. Subconsciously, *I can't be like that – it must be them*; At times like these, I realize I still have work to do on my own shadow side, the side that is difficult to face and acknowledge;
- How does it show up in different areas of your life? Is there someone you have a particularly hard time interacting with? What is it about them you are having difficulty with? Can you see this in yourself at times as well? What would it be like for you to be empathetic with the person versus judgmental? How might this change the dynamic in the moment and support you to respond to them in a more genuine way and with more compassion?
- When we learn to see the goodness in people and have compassion for them, to stay with our curious-self versus reacting with judgment, we actually give ourselves a gift because through learning to be kinder to them, we learn to be kinder to ourselves;
- If the word compassionate is loaded for you, or if you have judgments about it and it feels uncomfortable, think about it as empathy, the ability to step into another's shoes and understand their experience. While

you may not totally agree with what someone else believes, you can still endeavour to understand it. This, in turn, takes away the stigma affiliated with their circumstances;
- Through a shift in how we think about the world and ourselves, we can learn to live with the inner critic, or befriend it, so it allows us to be who we truly are and not who we have learned to be.

The Arc of Intense Energy is an effective tool supporting you to recognize and manage the inner critic:

- Through developing self-awareness, learning to rebalance our thoughts, and opening to a new voice, one of compassion and empathy, over time, we are able to turn down the volume of the inner critic and let go of its hold. This provides us with more choice, and we can respond versus react; see the Arc of Intense Energy in Conversation 1;
- No matter where we are, the inner critic can stop us from saying what we really what to say or do what we really want to do; it may say, *That's stupid, don't say it, He's not going to agree, so why bother, I don't belong, That's wrong; it can only be one way, and that's this way*;
- It may take us to judgment when we feel we are not being accepted, loved, respected or valued. We can then become an inner critic for others as our mindset takes us away from being empathetic or compassionate towards others, and we feel we need to protect ourselves from someone else's way of being that is not in line with ours; *He's so aggressive , or she's so condescending* when the reason may be that they've had a really bad morning and being empathetic would calm the situation down. Remember that everyone has their own story and their own inner critic. Not everyone is on the same path of self-awareness and personal growth;
- Or maybe, we need to be gentler with ourselves by honouring who we are within these moments by stepping back, taking a breath, and speaking our truth, responding authentically instead of reacting inauthentically.

Judgments can be created through projections:

As mentioned above, one of the things that can occur when critical of others and making judgments, is that the inner critic is misplaced on to them. This is called *projection*. You project something onto the person you judge when it is too uncomfortable to see the same in yourself. For example, *thinking that person is so loud and talks a lot versus having personal awareness that you can also be loud and talk too much. Becoming aware of these parts of yourself and accepting them can help to develop compassion or empathy for yourself and others.*

Arc of Intense Energy Writing Reflection:

Refer to the diagram and description of the Arc of Intense Energy in Conversation 1. Reflect on the topic of this Conversation - *Discovering More About Yourself By Managing The Inner Critic*. Answer the following questions in order to understand how the *Arc* is showing up for you:

What is your old, automatic pattern when triggered? Where is your inner critical voice triggering you? For example, *when I am triggered by someone's expression when I voice how I feel, I immediately begin to defend those emotions:*

What is a new behaviour, belief or attitude you would like to choose instead? For example, *in that same scenario, I can choose to slow down and take the time to ask that person what they are thinking about the emotions and thoughts I shared:*

Practice self-managing through the *Arc* when you are moving through your day and while in your caregiving role or when spending time alone. Begin by paying attention, noticing the energy or discomfort intensifying in the body. As this occurs, practice relaxing your shoulders and belly and deepen and slow your breathing.

This will allow you to feel the emotions as they arise, notice your thoughts and determine if they are aligned with your values or just old, unhelpful messages.

When you discover which is true and right, you will be able to maintain your perspective and choose an appropriate and authentic response for the situation at hand. And, you will become decisive in the way you choose to live…for now.

After a few weeks of practicing, reflect on what you are learning and how you will adjust your thoughts and behaviours as a result.

Resources
Loving What Is, Byron Katie. | Taming Your Gremlin, Rick Carson.

Action Steps

Exercise:

Answer the Following Questions to Get to Know Your Inner Critic a Bit Better:

- What does your inner critic sound like? Is it high pitched, low volume, soft, loud, etc.? Or do you sense it as a feeling? If so, describe the feeling:

- What does your inner critic look like? Is it an angry schoolmaster, a monster, a troll, your mother, father, etc.?

- When you are journaling, what are the messages your inner critic is saying to you; That's stupid! Who do you think you are? You have nothing of interest to say to others. You are too old to start this new path. Why do you want to uncover secrets and memories that will be painful?

- How are these messages impacting your life as you chose to create a new self-care routine and communicate to yourself while continuing to support your loved one?

- What would it be like if you lived free of this inner critical voice most of the time?

What is one thing you are learning about yourself? What is one thing you can you do differently as you continue to grow within your own self-discovery while listening to your inner voice?

Reflections:

When you begin working with the inner critic, you learn to create a different way of thinking about your life - imagine re-hardwiring your brain to a new way that may feel uncomfortable if your automatic pattern is to adopt a negative perspective most of the time. Give yourself a chance. Remember, like so many others, it will take time and self-compassion as you begin using practices to become aware of what you choose to pay attention to and begin rebalancing your thoughts.

- Write down exactly what it is saying to you and how you feel as a result. Your inner critic is saying the following right now: For example, You are spending too much time on yourself; you need to be taking care of others:

- Write down an alternative, more balanced message for yourself. A more balanced way for you to think about this situation is the following: For example, The more connected I feel to my inner-self, the more balanced I feel. I have more of myself to share with those I love more compassionately and authentically:

- Notice how each of these statements feels when you re-read them. It is important to begin to notice how the inner critic impacts you physically so you can learn to notice it, let it go, and move on -The Arc of Intense Energy:

    - When you read the inner critic's statement, you feel:

    - When you read the more balanced statement, you feel:

- Ask yourself how you would interpret these messages from authentic-self, without the impacts of your critical voice. Listen to your intuition regarding what your truth is in the situation. Re-interpret it using this perspective and use your values and Inner Purpose Feeling to guide you through this process. Then, notice how clarity provides you with the confidence to let your inner critic go…for now. For example, I am learning that I often don't set a boundary or I say yes when I am feeling I don't have the energy or emotional clarity in the moment. I really want to say, "I can't do what you are asking of me at this moment." When I don't listen to myself, I end up in a situation where I resent what is being asked of me or angry for not standing up for myself and my needs in the moment. If I am honest and have a conversation around how I am feeling and what I am capable of at that time, there is an opportunity to have a discussion and come to a compromise or a different way to get what needs to be done:

- When you listen to your intuition and are aware of your inner critic or the more emotionally mature way to interpret this situation, you find the more balanced or objective way to think about this situation is:

Continued Daily Practices to Support Managing Your Inner Critic Through Journaling:

Review the foundational practices you have been committing to. If you feel comfortable with all of them, continue including them in your daily routine. However, if you are not resonating with one or more, take the time to discover what you prefer practicing to create a mindset that promotes physical, emotional, and spiritual presence.

Stick with the free-flow activities you have been enjoying. If you have space, feel free to add a different activity or switch any out for another like gardening.

What's Next? Have a Conversation With Your Soul Through Journaling:

What is your soul saying to you about your inner critic? How are you feeling about managing your inner critic, and how can you express this through journaling – having a conversation with your soul? Grab your journal and write what you are discovering about yourself.

A Conversation With My Soul
By Donna Fitzgerald

My Door to Freedom was Facing Fear

I lived most of my life unaware that fear was such a part of it. It wasn't until I began my path of self-discovery after a traumatic event in my life that this awareness presented itself. I started to journal and heal from loss and grief from caregiver burnout and the death of my husband. I came to the awareness that fear had many faces in my life.

In my childhood, because of sexual abuse, I was afraid people would find out my secret. Fear presented itself by my being extremely shy, feeling awkward, ugly and invisible.

As a teenager, I was afraid of joining groups or sports in high school for fear of failure and being laughed at. I feared of being noticed and was very insecure, and I became a target for being teased by the boys at school.

As a wife and mother, I tried to be perfect and be the best I could be for fear of not measuring up. I felt like I had nothing to say. I knew my place in the adult world and what was expected of me. I quietly moved through life unseen.

The door to freedom began to open-up when I pushed to meet fear, move outside my comfort zone, and challenge it. This came from my new daily journaling as I began to challenge my thoughts and feelings.

I remember the first time I stood in front of a group of co-workers at a retirement party to present a gift to a co-worker who was retiring. I was terrified. What would I say? Will I cry? Will I pass out? All these thoughts danced around in my head and my heart beat so fast that I thought it was going to jump out of my chest. I presented the gift and none of the fears I had in my head came to light, and I felt wonderful. I did it! I now had proof that maybe the thoughts I was telling myself were not true.

I have experienced hundreds of battles with fear over the past ten years. Some have been significant, and some have been small. I learned to challenge the emotional feeling and physical sensation that arises when experiencing something new, or meeting new people, and traveling.

I now ask myself questions when I feel fear. Why am I afraid? Is this going to hurt me? Am I going to grow and learn from this experience? Once I answer them all and find clarity about the situation, I can jump in, and I don't look back.

Fear is taking a backseat in my life. I live life now. I have met wonderful people, travelled to Australia on my own for the first time, tried speed skating, ran a 30-kilometre run. I am 56 and training this summer for my first sprint triathlon. I am already a winner because I have faced my fear and am enjoying every day and the process of challenging my body and mind.

Fear will always be a part of my life but it does not stop me anymore, knowing that fear gives me the confidence and courage to move through my life to experience every day with excitement and gratitude.

Freedom is what I feel when I have an open heart, courage, and curiosity to say to life, Bring it On!

Creating What Inner Balance Feels Like For You

Journaling Through Conversation 6

Determining what inner balance feels like for you.

How can you consciously create inner balance to inspire journaling and self-discovery?

The following worksheet will assist you in understanding what inner balance feels like for you.
It will help you take the first steps to make adjustments when you feel out of balance.
Often, when moving through caregiving and discovering more about yourself,
there are times when you may feel your inner balance being compromised.
This is when you can reflect on the Arc of Intense Energy and how having clarity about your
personality, values, Inner Purpose Feeling, and inner critic messages
can guide you towards the awareness you need to re-balance.

Things to Consider About What Inner Balance Is:

- A state of being that evolves from knowing your emotions and feelings;
- A mindset that develops allowing you to trust how you feel or intuitively know;
- A choice you make when the inner critic attempts to create chaos;
- A muscle you can strengthen and a life-long practice;
- A first step supporting you towards living authentically in all areas of your life.

Inner Balance is a state of being that evolves from knowing your emotions and feelings:

Think of a hurricane where the storm of life frantically whirls, and inside the clouds, there is the eye. There is calm in the eye, but that doesn't mean the storm has stopped or slowed in intensity – on the contrary, the storm may continue for some time.

This concept is discussed in a book called *Slowing Down to the Speed of Life*. The authors describe two modes of thinking – the processing, analytical or task mode and the free-flow mode described as creative intelligence or effortless thinking.[6] They talk about how important it is to learn to balance and live in both modes in order to live more effectively. Western culture values and rewards the *getting things done* mode of processing, so you learn to spend a large part of your life living in this way of thinking. When you re-learn spending time in the free-flow mode, you can tap more fully into your creativity, wisdom, and original thinking.

Defining balance is a tricky thing because everyone's perception of a balanced state of being is different. Knowing your emotions and feelings requires clarifying your authentic way of being – who you are when choosing what you say, what you do, and how you respond to others and situations from your essence. This, in turn, requires a deep knowing of which characteristics resonate with you – review what you learned about your Enneagram Type in Conversation 1 - so you have the choice to show up within those that serve you well. When you choose to assess the behaviours of others and everything around you, you can establish how you want to respond to them authentically, and that provides you with a balanced inner state of being, or inner balance – you can show up in a way that is in line with your personal integrity.

When reflecting on your Enneagram personality type, you will notice that the characteristics it describes can influence your unique experience of inner balance. For example, the Peacemaker, number 9, values characteristics of being calm and peaceful and will likely be drawn to a different state of inner balance than the Enthusiast, number 7, who values characteristics of spontaneity and being energized. Each exhibits a very different external picture.

I am at my best when I am calm and peaceful within myself. I need structure and know what needs to be done to keep everyone in my life happy and healthy. As I follow my self-care routine, I feel energized and have the focus and drive to meet the tasks of the day. I don't require much contact with others as I find being in the presence of too many people drains my energy. I set healthy boundaries to help me manage my daily living; this is when I am healthiest. If I don't set boundaries with my time and need for self-care, I find myself out of balance and over-giving.
The truth is that I am a highly energetic person, and when I enjoy what I am doing and focus on what I am passionate about, it feeds my soul, and I feel connected to something much greater than myself. This is when I feel in balance – when I honour who I am as my best self. I have a quiet voice, and I am passionate about making a difference in the lives of those who are experiencing caregiver burnout, loss of self, and grief. I feel connected and of service when I share my wisdom and life experiences with others to help them discover their own self-care routines.

---

[6] Richard Carlson and Joseph Bailey, Slowing Down to the Speed of Life – How to create a more peaceful, simpler life from the Inside out, pp. 11 – 15.

Inner balance is a mindset that allows you to trust how you feel or intuitively know:

When referring to balance, you may assume the conversation will entail an exercise describing the practice of balancing areas of your life. However, I encourage you to dig deeper than that and reflect on your values, and even deeper to be curious about your values' feelings or an intuitive knowing. Are you living in line with each of your values most of the time? Are you using the IPF process – review Conversation 4 -tapping into your Inner Purpose Feeling steps to guide you towards a balanced state of mind and being? This is inner balance, and it is different for everyone. The awareness of yours is essential to feeling balanced from the inside-out. Time spent journaling will help you intuitively know how it feels to be balanced from what is revealed. The Arc of Intense Energy - reflecting on how you feel, both physically and emotionally - is another tool for creating changes in your way of being.

Using your customized values' feelings and your Inner Purpose Feeling can also influence what inner balance means to you. For example, if one of your values is *adventure*, your IPF may be excitement. However, if you value *solitude*, your IPF may be *calm*. When you manage your inner-self guided by these feelings and, in particular, your Inner Purpose Feeling, you naturally make decisions that create ease of *being* and then *doing*. This process then translates into outer life balance as your feelings transition into thoughts of what you want to do, say, and how you want to be. As an example, my Inner Purpose Feeling is *Calm*, and being respectful of others' emotions and understanding them provides me with a sense of connection to them and to my soul; this provides me with a balanced state of calm. If I feel disconnected at any time, I take a step back and reflect on why – this is the Arc of Intense Energy process. I can usually gain clarity through my journaling practice. I can confidently make a choice that takes me back to feeling calm. Things that make me feel disconnected are the following: when I don't set healthy boundaries (resentful), maintain my self-care routine (lethargic and isolated), don't speak my truth (invisible), don't express myself creatively (stuck). When I am aware of these uncomfortable feelings, I can step back and think about why, and then choose a different way – towards a comfortable, balanced way that includes feelings of confidence, strength, being seen and inspired, etc. These values' feelings are experienced through my caregiver role or through understanding myself better. For Example, While I was caregiving and working full time, I felt exhausted and pushed through the fatigue. I knew intuitively I needed rest but ignored the warning. I went to work one day and couldn't find my purse. I had security look for it, and I was panicked. I looked in the drawer several times without seeing it. It was found in the drawer by a co-worker. I was not processing information because I was going on adrenaline while facing setting up respite for my husband to allow me time to rest. My inner critic told me, *you have to do everything*, while my feelings and intuition told me *you need rest because you have not slept through the night in two years.*

Inner balance is a choice you make when the inner critic attempts to create chaos:

The inner critic can wreak havoc on your state of inner balance as it often sends messages asking you to do more and speed up your mind. If you listen to this voice, you will get side-tracked and avoid or block your feelings. With greater awareness of how this impacts your decision-making, you will be able to respond authentically to situations and others in a balanced way that feels right for you. Knowing your inner critic and its motives will allow you to evaluate whether it supports your inner balance or tries to sabotage it. You have a keen awareness of what resonates with you at this point, so knowing you have the power to be guided by your truth will support you to choose balance over chaos confidently; clarity is the key to creating it - rather than doing what your critic expects you to. For example: When I realized I was experiencing caregiver burnout, my inner critic told me others would judge me if I took time for myself to rest.

However, my body physically warned me that I needed to make changes, or I would not be able to care for my husband, children, or myself. I chose to listen to my intuition and ignore my inner critic, making changes in my daily caregiving routine and self-care to become more balanced and present in all the roles in my life at the time.

Balance is a *Muscle* You Learn to Strengthen Over Time:

One difference between those who manage inner and outer balance effectively, and those who don't, is that *balanced* individuals are perceived to be outwardly calm; you will get a sense of this when you meet them. While they may be busy, they are not anxious or overwhelmed, at least not a lot of the time. They have figured out what it takes to live life from a place where, when they feel frantic, they can assess their state of being with their values and IPF as guides. They can then choose not to be in it, or when to be in it and when to step back to regain perspective. They can navigate towards what makes them feel centred and that organically motivates them to care for themselves, manage stress effectively, and be consistent within their personal foundation with the caveat that there are times when they move towards imbalance. These people have learned to notice when this happens, to navigate tradeoffs and return to a sense of both inner and outer balance more quickly than those who have not. Long-term stress has many implications when it comes to feeling internally chaotic and showing up outwardly overwhelmed. It also has implications for the immune system, cardiovascular disease and other health-related issues.

When you find yourself experiencing signs of stress in thinking, behavior, or mood, you may:

- Become irritable and intolerant of even minor disturbances;
- Feel irritated or frustrated, lose your temper more often;
- Feel jumpy or exhausted all the time;
- Find it hard to concentrate or focus on tasks;
- Worry too much about insignificant things;
- Doubt your ability to do things;
- Imagine negative, worrisome, or terrifying scenes;
- Feel you are missing opportunities because you cannot act quickly enough.[8]

In order to experience less stress and imbalance, maintaining emotional and physical balance in all areas of self is imperative to being healthy and empowered. Using your values' feelings to achieve inner balance will influence how balanced you will feel externally.

---

[7] Ibid.
[8] Source: http://www.webmd.com/balance/stress-management/stress-management-effects-of-stress

Arc of Intense Energy Reflection:

Refer to the diagram and description of the Arc of Intense Energy in Conversation 1. Reflect on the topic of this chapter – *Creating What Inner Balance Feels Like For You*. Answer the following questions to understand how the Arc is showing up for you:

What is your old, automatic pattern when triggered? For example, *My old pattern was to put my family's needs ahead of my own. I had guilt around putting my needs ahead of others. I was the one who was keeping my family happy and healthy my needs weren't important:*

What is a new behaviour, belief or attitude you would like to choose instead? For example, *Once I realized that I needed to put my own needs first and create time to start a new daily practice, including sleep, nutrition, exercise and emotional well-being, I was more equipped to handle the daily tasks that my caregiving role required:*

Practice self-managing through the *Arc* when you are learning about living true to your values. Begin by paying attention, noticing the energy or discomfort intensifying in the body. As this occurs, practice relaxing your shoulders and belly and deepen and slow your breathing.
This will allow you to feel the emotions as they arise, notice your thoughts and determine if they are aligned with your values or just old, unhelpful messages. Write about these emotions and thoughts in your journal.

When you learn to understand what is true and right, you will be able to articulate and understand how to respond to uncomfortable situations in life. While caregiving, you will feel intense emotions, but you will be able to determine where they are coming from and make decisions that serve both you and your loved one. For example, your *Arc* may be presenting from a place of personal fatigue or frustration within a caregiving situation.

By managing the *Arc* through journaling, you will be able to find a new self-awareness about what to do next while shifting old patterns and thoughts.

Action Steps

Exercise:

Complete this exercise to get a sense of your current state of inner balance:

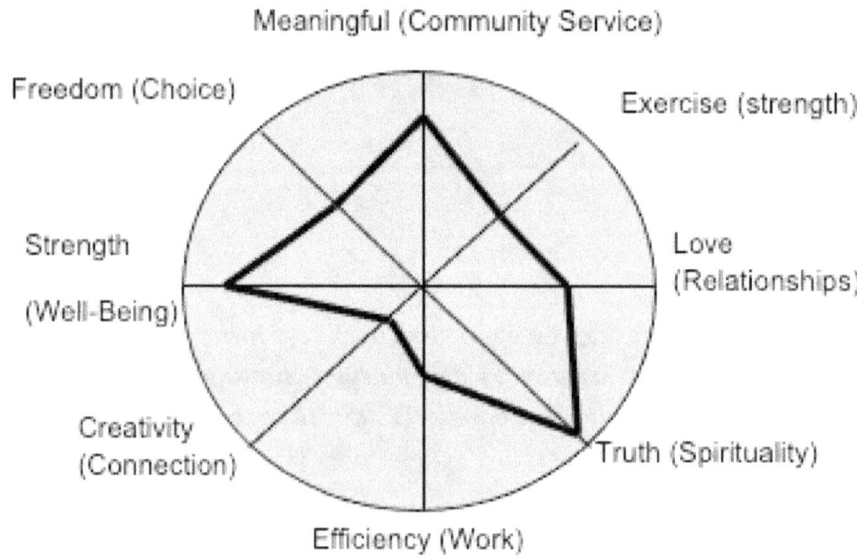

Example of one person's current inner balance:

Simply, this diagram shows the different parts of this person's Inner Purpose Feeling - 8 values and their associated feelings. It also shows where they chose to measure them based on how much effort and energy they are currently spending living in line with each of them. The outside of the circle is the optimal level, and the point they chose on each line corresponding with the value; it indicates their current level of commitment to it.

It gives an idea about which area(s) they may be feeling out of balance and want to make adjustments in. In the example, this person is happy with the energy and time they are spending on feeling meaningful, truth, and strength. One area they might want to focus on is feeling efficient. Or maybe they actually don't....

What is important is that we don't obsess about the imperfection of what our state of inner balance is at any time. It would be unreasonable to think that our balance diagram could ever be equally measured at any one point in our life. Be compassionate with yourself as you recognize that perfection is unrealistic and unattainable. It is natural that one unbalanced area of ourselves, one value, will affect other areas, a number of values, as we attempt to do the best we can. Sometimes we need to be out of balance in one area, one value, to focus more on others and what is important to us at that time. Being aware of what is a priority is what needs to be top of mind.

Using the instructions below, complete the following inner balance diagram to get a sense of your current state of balance:

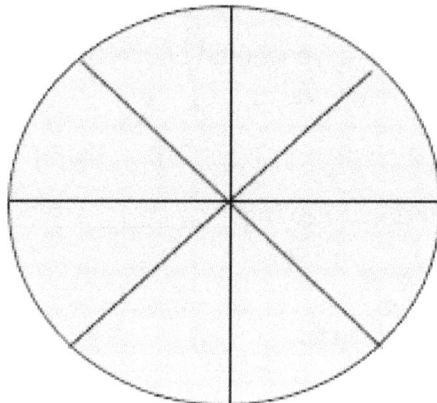

Instructions for completing your inner balance diagram:

- Take the first 8 top values' feeling words you determined in Conversation 3 and write one on each line within the wheel;
- Assume the outer edge of the circle is the optimal level you are currently living guided by each value, and the centre of the circle is the less than ideal level;
- Place a dot on the line for each component/value to show where you feel you would currently land;
- For example, you want to experience feeling your definition of effectiveness in your work, and the job you have provides you with this opportunity most of the time – you will likely place a dot closer to the outer edge;
- Or, you want to experience feeling your definition of love within your relationship with your partner, but you are feeling disconnected from them lately – you will likely place a dot closer to the inner circle;
- Once you have a dot on each line, join them with a line to provide a visual of your current inner balance;
- Reflect on what this tells you as you become more self-aware. Think about what adjustments you might want to make in your way of thinking and living to, if any, shift the balance to the one you are comfortable with. It is important to recognize that there is seldom anyone who is perfectly balanced as we are constantly recalibrating life and our perception of it.

Reflections:

Reflections about my current versus optimal inner balance:

Given your current balance, one value/feeling you would like to adjust to achieve more balance would be: For example, *Work as the value, and Efficient as the feeling.*

Value _____   Emotional Feeling _____.

Consider the realities of making adjustments:

- What are the realities when you consider the decisions you are currently making that compromise the value above? What do you need to do, or what mindset/belief do you need to shift to live more in line with that value and create more balance in your life. For example: *When my value of wellness and feeling strong is compromised by putting all my energy into my caregiver role needs, I create an unhealthy expectation for my own self-care. I become resentful because my needs aren't being seen or met:*

- How could you think through all the possible solutions? Who could support you? For example, *I need to partner with my inner critic and reflect on what it is saying to me, so I can ask for more help and direction within my caregiver role to free up time to allow for my own needs and wellness to be more in balance:*

- What will the trade-offs be if you make adjustments, and how can your values help you decide the right way to make the adjustment? For example, *I am navigating the trade-offs associated with a possible respite admission for my loved one for a few weeks. I know their needs will be met while I spend time getting the sleep I require and the support to make informed decisions that are the best for myself and my loved one. While I move through another stage of my caregiving role, I use my daily journaling to assist me in knowing what my emotions are expressing:*

- What might be challenging in making changes to create more inner balance? For example, *I may have to face the reality that I can no longer look after my loved one on a full-time basis. Also, the changes needed for my self-care will be made, so I can experience more quality time, as opposed to more quantity of time being exhausted and risking burn-out:*

- What support might you need? Who could you ask for support?

- What conversations do you need to have?

Building the skills and confidence for having uncomfortable conversations is one of the most important skills for practicing inner and outer balance. They may be needed to navigate through new situations and brainstorm new possibilities and ways of thinking and being.

Reflect on your top values from Conversation 3. How can they support you in feeling more outer balance?

- What are three to five words that describe your core values? For example, *work, relationships, creativity, inclusion, personal evolution:*

- What are the values feelings you chose to describe the emotions you experience when living in line with them? For example, *effectiveness - work, love - relationships, creativity - truth, ease - inclusion, wisdom - personal evolution:*

- How can these values' feelings guide me in making trade-offs in order to have more outer balance in my life? For example, *If I value self-care, I will choose to manage my time, allowing me to connect with myself and regularly meet my needs - knowing that there will be times while caregiving when this is not possible, but will allow me the choice to move between the two to create balance:*

Continued Daily Practices to Support Inner and Outer Balance Through Journaling:

Review the foundational practices you have been committing to. If you feel comfortable with all of them, continue including them in your daily routine. However, if you are not resonating with one or more, take the time to discover what you prefer practicing to create a mindset that promotes physical, emotional, and spiritual presence. If you have too many things going on, feel free to drop one to make space for rest.

Stick with the free-flow activities you have been enjoying. If you have space, feel free to add a different activity or switch any out for another like painting.

What's Next? Have a Conversation With Your Soul Through Journaling:

What is your soul saying to you about what your inner balance feels like for you? How are you feeling about shifting some things around in your life, and how can you express this through journaling – having a conversation with your soul? Grab your journal and write what you are discovering about yourself.

A Conversation With My Soul
By Donna Fitzgerald

What is My Inner Light?

My inner light is my soul. The part of me that lives deep within my being. The voice that speaks to me. The part of me that was locked away for many years. The soul I was born with that came into the world shining bright with the light of God. The mystery of life to be lived through the innocence of a child.

My light was diminished to a mere flicker as sexual abuse entered my life when I was little girl. The scared little girl who had a big secret, was shy, and felt ugly and alone. It wasn't until I was in my 40's when I realized I had locked away my light many years before to protect my soul.

The catalyst to changed was a traumatic event that happened while I was caregiving for my husband through his ALS diagnosis. This experience opened the door to my childhood sexual abuse and it blew open during an intimate moment with my husband. The pleading eyes I saw were not his; they were the eyes of my abuser, my father. I was horrified, having to deal with the impending death of my husband and the now an awakened secret of the past. I was confused, questioning everything in my life. Where did I go? Who am I? What do I do now? How can I do this?

My answer was to choose life, not grief. There was a little voice within that nudged me to move forward, telling me to be the best I could be. The choice was mine to listen to my inner voice, my intuition, or ignore the voice and stay in the pain, grief as a victim. That small glimmer of light the little girl lost had a chance to be heard. I started making small changes one step at a time, and my first lesson was that no one could do the work for me. I was the only one who could find Donna. I had to acknowledge the pain of the dark secret of abuse and the pain of watching my husband die from ALS. I had to learn to be alone with my thoughts and emotions. I had to allow the tears to flow and journal the pain, loss, and fear onto paper as I gave my past a voice. I grew up with the notion that I was to be seen and not heard. The little girl within me had held this secret for over forty years. I had protected the secret and myself. The more I expressed myself on paper, I realized I have a voice and something to say. I wrote a letter and found the courage to face my father and read my truth to him. I found the strength to conquer my fears, to challenge the untruths that kept me from shining bright with love, hope, and confidence.

I have been on my path of self-discovery now for over ten years, and as I gain more self-awareness my light shines brighter every day. I have done this through journaling, meditating, taking care of myself.

I can now look in the mirror and see the amazing woman I am. I can look myself in the eyes and see who I am. I don't need anyone to tell me I am worthy, beautiful, and loving; I have learned that the most amazing lesson in life is to love myself, all of me, and that I am enough. I dug deep through tears and life's lessons to gain confidence and trust my inner voice, my soul, my light.

I have taken my power back, and I know that I am the only one who can give it away. I am free to be ME! There is no need to go through life protecting my heart, living in fear of others judging me if they know my story. Every day is a new adventure, and having been given the gift of life, I will never take it for granted.

My light will shine brightly and continue to grow more magnificent every day for the rest of my life until the day I go to meet that great light in the afterlife.

My light shines as bright as the sun on a summer's day and the full moon in the midnight sky.

I am light! I am love! I am Me!

Setting Personal Boundaries To Express Your Truth

Journaling Through Conversation 7

Setting boundaries to express your truth with confidence and ease.

How can you create boundaries to support self-care while caregiving?

The following worksheet will help you begin practicing how to create personal boundaries to live an authentic life while caring for your loved one and supporting your own personal growth. Creating boundaries through grief or the loss of a loved one will allow you to become more aware of your emotions and feelings through self-discovery. First, I will provide context about how to think about boundaries and then provide actual steps to begin setting your own. In addition, I will refer to earlier conversations and concepts to begin tying them all together.

Things to Consider When Setting Personal Boundaries To Express Your Truth:

- Slowing and listening to your body, emotions, and feelings to support knowing when you are prioritizing something other than what you need or want;
- Clarifying what is acceptable to you to set personal boundaries, using your values as guideposts – a reminder of the role of your values and Inner Purpose Feeling;
- Understanding the interplay between over-functioning and anger - a reminder of the role of the inner critic;
- Understanding that it doesn't need to be one way or the other – a reminder of the role of determining inner balance;
- Compassion is key as you learn a new way – a reminder of the role of having authentic conversations with your soul and with others.

Slowing and listening to your body, emotions, and feelings to support knowing when you are prioritizing something other than what you need or want:

- Being able to feel and express your emotions, particularly anger and resentment, is not easy. It may take an event in your life like illness, trauma, or grief that acts as a catalyst to change. You may be faced with choices to help you move through what life gives you. This is why learning to listen to the signals your body provides you is so important. This brings us back to the Arc of Intense Energy and the importance of taking the time to feel your physical and then emotional responses to what you experience to make decisions based on what you truly need and want. This new awareness can be very uncomfortable in the beginning. The more you grow within yourself, you will understand and move through these emotions with more ease;
- What would it be like for you to pause and wait before immediately saying yes and adding something to your day that is solely to please another person? How would it feel to take that moment to make space and think about what you really want to do before accommodating someone else?
- Think of something you want to accomplish for yourself. Now, sit back and review the day you have planned and determine where you could fit a few moments into journaling, go for a walk in nature, read a book, listen to music, something that is just for you. What do you feel physically as you take the time to sit in the space, providing you with the choice to determine how you can move forward?
- Perhaps you feel tension because your thoughts go to your default of the perception that you should put others' needs ahead of yours and you are unworthy. Or you relax into your body and breathe through any tension from within you as you shift your belief to one that honours your needs and your worthiness;
- What emotions arise during these moments of slowing down while thinking about what you want and how to create it? You might feel anxious, resentful, and angry as you hang on to the belief that you don't have time to make yourself a priority. Or you might feel calm, excited, and confident, knowing there is a way to respect your needs without letting others down – it may just have to be done a different way. For Example: *When I acknowledged my fatigue, mind fog, and my chaotic emotions and feelings, I realized I was experiencing caregiver burnout. I had to make changes in my life to support my health. If I didn't put my needs and health on the list, I would not be able to care for anyone. I still had my caregiving, parenting, working, and other responsibilities. With my new self-awareness through my journaling and learning about my values and Inner Purpose Feeling, I knew that changes had to be made to create a more balanced life. My husband went into long term care, and I brought him home on weekends. I started a new exercise routine to regain my physical strength, and I could now sleep through the night four days a week. I was creating space for new foundational practices that would support me moving forward in my life. I was more rested and present when my husband came home on the weekend:*

Clarifying what is acceptable to you to set personal boundaries using your values as guideposts – a reminder of the role of your values and Inner Purpose Feeling:

You can learn how to use your values to set personal boundaries. Values are deeply held beliefs about what is important to you and how you want to live, so they are, essentially, your bottom line. As a result, you can use them to establish what is acceptable to you and what is not.

You articulated your values and the feelings you associate with them in Conversation 3; keep them with you and use them as guideposts for decision-making. Share your values and Inner Purpose Feeling with others and have an authentic conversation about them with others. This entails using your self-awareness to help deepen your commitment to your core values and allows others to understand them and why you make the choices you do.

You are making changes to how you show up in the world, and those who know you will notice the difference. Some may not understand why you are choosing to be more authentic and may need time to accept these changes. Being open and honest about why you need to make these changes will help others understand, and they may offer to help in ways that you have not thought of.

Your values and IPF support you to make decisions and set boundaries that define what is acceptable to you and what is not. They validate your priorities and support you to move in the direction of a more balanced life that supports everyone.

There may be times when you become unclear about what your boundaries look like. If you do not allow yourself to feel your emotions and establish which one of your values is being compromised, you may just experience the situation as something that isn't working for you or something that feels weird and can't be explained. When you begin opening to feeling your emotions, you become aware of the signals that can support you to take a step back as you experience those uncomfortable emotions. You can then shift from unconscious habits and unhealthy personality characteristics and make conscious shifts towards what is right for you, and in line with your values. Going back to review your Enneagram Personality description can help determine which characteristics serve you well and which do not. For example, *My Enneagram personality is the Peacemaker. I am at my best when I feel inner-stability and peace of mind. Knowing that everyone around me is okay. When I am out of balance, I feel overwhelmed that I am not able to maintain balance in the lives of those around me. I have to implement my foundational practices to help me gain more clarity and balance. So, when I felt tightness in my chest and experienced guilt when breaking a promise made very early on in my husband's diagnosis, I felt upset with myself for not being able to follow through on a promise. I had this unrealistic expectation that I could do everything well and take care of everyone's needs, not knowing the progression of his disease would take years, not months. I have since learned that my value of wellness was not in line with the choices I made. I was putting all my energy into my family and forgetting that, without being healthy and well, I would not be able to support the needs of them or myself. It was when I hit my breaking point that I truly understood what it felt like to not know Donna. I had disappeared. Taking the time to journal and spend time with me, I realized that the time spent within my caregiver responsibilities might have to change on the outside, but the love for my husband and family did not have to change. I knew the changes I was making were to support my family; to be strong for my children and have the strength to move through grief after my husband's death and to create a new life as a single parent. I understood that not everyone in my life would understand and some might fall away from my circle of friends. Those who remained are the ones that love me unconditionally.*

As you support yourself to think and speak your truth and do what you really want, you build your self-worth. It becomes an amplified feeling of confidence that builds and builds while you, simultaneously, undo old habits and belief systems you created long ago.

Over-functioning[9] and anger – a reminder of the role of the inner critic:

You might have a subconscious belief that self-esteem is achieved by getting others to like you, that you feel worthy because you believe that doing things for others puts you in a more positive light. Conversely, you can also establish a belief system that others will feel negatively towards you if you create boundaries around how much you support them, and instead, focus on what you love in life. The result is an adopted pattern or habit of *over-functioning* or doing more for others than is required or they do for you. This behaviour shows up if you listen to particular inner critic messages that influence the belief that you must support others' aspirations before making space for your own.

This dominoes into saying *yes* to others when asked and falling into the trap of automatically doing things for them due to years of established patterning. Because a mindset of an expectation of loyalty is developed, you continuously do whatever makes them happy. More often than not, the people you are bending over backwards for have no expectation at all. It's just a story you may have made up from patterns in your mind experienced over and over again.

If you continue to give your time and energy to others without providing yourself with the same, you will see them achieve what they want while you do not, and resentment can build. In your mind, you see them *under-functioning* or doing less for you than you expect of them and getting ahead, while you *over-function* without fulfilling your dreams. It's not that you want them to do more for you or over-function as you are, but you become frustrated that you are not experiencing the same level of purpose and fulfillment they are – they feel confident and worthy, and you feel insecure and unworthy. The inner critic takes the lead.

People who over-function usually don't tell others what they want or ask for the support they require. They continue to commit to doing anything others need to make them happy. They may become annoyed with those who choose to set personal boundaries that they are unable to. This can transition into feelings of resentment and then anger. If that anger is suppressed, the cycle continues; they continue to fulfill others' expectations, whether real or made up. That anger eventually comes out in one way or another. Yet, the pattern of over-functioning continues because they do not break the cycle by setting personal boundaries to achieve what they want.

For example, *throughout my life, until my mid-forties, when I experienced caregiver burnout and loss of self, I was seen and not heard. As a child, I was the good girl, always doing what she was told, whether at home or school. I always said yes and did what was asked of me. These patterns were formed very early in my childhood. When I got married in my early twenties, I took the role of wife and mother very seriously and I did it perfectly. I worked at a job where I always said yes, regardless if I was already stretched. I took on more responsibilities both at home and work. I was not aware of values, the Inner Purpose Feeling or inner critic - that was not something I thought*

---

[9] Harriet Lerner, Ph.D., The Dance of Anger – A Woman's Guide to Changing the Patterns of Intimate Relationships, Note, while this book focuses on these patterns for women, the principles apply to both men and women.

of or even knew existed; I was living my life as I had when I was a child. The problem with living from a place of unhealthy beliefs and patterns was that they were magnified when my husband was diagnosed with ALS and I took on the added caregiving to all the other responsibilities. There were offers of help, but I thought I was the only one who could truly look after him. I knew him best. After four years of this unrealistic pace of life working full-time, caregiving, parenting, and the stresses of everyday life, I found the cracks starting to show. I was not performing at work as I once did, coworkers were complaining about my work, home life was in crisis, our children were feeling the anxiety and anger my husband was experiencing with the loss of control within his own life. I was juggling everyone's breakdowns, thankfully not all on the same day. I was over functioning. In a split second, on a day that was particularly difficult, I saw my 10-year-old daughter hiding in the corner as my husband had a meltdown. I saw her out of the corner of my eye. I knew at that moment that changes had to be made - this was about my children, not about me. We were all fighting to keep life as normal as possible, and we were all angry that this disease was changing our daily life on a regular basis.

I was grateful at this point in our family's journey as I started the process of journaling and therapy. I understood the importance of setting boundaries and listening to my body and emotions and feelings to help the situation. Even today, I am so grateful for the time we spent all together at home and the decisions we made. Through self-discovery, I found the importance of self-care and boundaries that are so important as life has its challenges, maintaining balance to juggle responsibilities and my self-care routine.

Understanding that it doesn't need to be one way or the other – a reminder of the role of determining inner balance:

It is essential to recognize that it doesn't have to be one or the other. To believe that you can do whatever you want to achieve your goals while ignoring others' needs is unrealistic as it goes outside of human instinct and the value of most to love and support. What is imperative is that you take the time to find a way to accommodate your needs while also supporting others.

You may sometimes choose to compromise and give more to others because one or more of your values indicates it is the right thing for you to do. And yet, you may stand firm at other times and choose to be loyal to your belief system as you request support from them. Remembering that life is not right or wrong, easy or hard, or equal or unfair at any given time can motivate you to use your values to recalibrate within all the variables that life throws at you. Accepting that there will always be trade-offs is the key.

Do you feel the empowerment of worthiness or the discomfort of unworthiness? Are you feeling the expectation of someone else? Is it real or made up? Do you feel resentment building? Do you recognize that your inner balance is being compromised when you begin to lean towards fulfilling others' happiness over your own? Are feelings of overwhelm, resentment, and anger building within you? Reflect on these questions and write your thoughts in your journal.

Learning how to feel and express anger can help you practice balancing how much you do for others while making space for yourself. Many people have a tough time actually feeling anger, and some rarely take the time to acknowledge it. Because they push it down into their subconscious, it ends up manifesting in one way or another – doing everything for others and nothing for themselves or having unrealistic thoughts of being liked by all as opposed to being disliked by some. It may even show up in a passive-aggressive behaviour like talking about the people they are catering to behind their backs. The very people they spend years trying to please become those they eventually resent.

Once you learn to step back, be curious, and feel your anger, quite often, the flood gates you expected would open end up becoming emotions and thoughts that last just a short time and then go away. You may experience increased awareness, and a new spaciousness opens up as you feel, acknowledge, and release these emotions. As a result, you realize that anger is a healthy and important emotion for you to listen to, clarify, and respond to. You become calmer through feelings of clarity and inner balance.

It is also important to relax and be open to experiencing these sensations and feelings in different situations. For example, a feeling like anxiousness in the pit of your stomach can mean your intuition is giving you a signal – the beginning of the Arc of Intensity process. Once you learn to experience and interpret it, you will have additional information for navigating all sorts of decision-making situations in a balanced way and by implementing boundaries. For example: *While caregiving, there were times I felt angry and I thought I had no control over my situation. I felt like there was no way forward; I was stuck. The reality was that once I sat back and evaluated the situation, there was usually a different way to approach it, and although there may have been anger, fear, and anxiousness, this all left once steps were taken to create a different way to handle the situation. It required me being honest and open with the people in my life - to set boundaries, to ask for help and also understand that my husband had his emotions and feelings to work through himself. He also felt trapped within his disease and had limited ways of expressing himself.*

Compassion is the key - a reminder of the role of having authentic conversations with your soul and with others:

Giving yourself a break can lighten the load and give you the foundational support going forward.

Remember that building any new skill takes time and can feel uncomfortable at first. You may not always do it as well as you like at first, but you can reframe it to recognize that you are making progress. As you learn, especially in times of stress, you may go back to the old, developed way. When this occurs, you have the choice to be compassionate with yourself and reflect on how it felt and what you might do differently next time. You may need to re-experience the old way several times until you are finally *done with it* and ready for a shift. Because you can count on a next time, there will be lots of opportunities to practice. When you do, you may notice the resistance to override it and see the U-turn as a gift in life and the next opportunity to learn.

As you build capacity, situations that seemed ominous in the past will have less impact on your decision-making. You will be able to determine how to support yourself, others, and society in a way that honours everyone. Setting boundaries provides the opportunity to fulfill your purpose and live true to your authentic passion while honouring the same for others. When you decide to set a boundary, become aware of the momentary discomfort that might appear. Then, practice self-awareness and take the time to discover how you can move forward with confidence and ease as you advocate for yourself and others in the process. Use the awareness you have developed about your values and how you feel when living in line with them to make authentic decisions. Accept the questions your inner critic challenges you with and respond to them honestly. Take your new-found decision-making skills to practice inner balance with the intention to show up as an advocate of self and others as you strive for the happiness that is your birthright. Have the authentic conversation with your soul that is necessary to discover your truth and another with those in your life to create the boundaries that serve everyone. This will become your new way as you shift away from the old.

A Reflection:

As a caregiver, you have chosen to support and advocate for your loved one while they progress through their illness. You give your unconditional love to support your loved one. A role I would do again in a heartbeat. What I would do differently is set personal boundaries earlier in my caregiver role. Through my own caregiving journey, I learned the importance of my own needs while giving to those I love. Understanding the importance of my own emotional, physical health contributes positively to the care for my loved one. Also, understanding that the progression of a disease and circumstances are out of my control. However, I have control over how I connect with myself to reach the demands of everyday life in a more authentic way.

Unfortunately, with caregiving, days turn into weeks, and weeks into months, until years go by, and you may find yourself adding more roles to your already hectic life as your loved one requires more care. Or, you may take on the everyday duties they can no longer complete themself. You will have nudges from within your intuition that changes need to be made. Your inner critic, Conversation 5, makes itself heard, telling you all the reasons why you can't change your routine and what you are doing today. For example: *I can't make changes because I made promises to my loved one. If I start including myself and start making changes, people will judge me, or I will feel shame. I am the only one who can take care of my loved one's needs. I know him/her the best.* These are just some of the thoughts that keep you stuck - caregiving without boundaries - which puts you at risk for caregiver burnout and loss of self.

Over the course of your life, you may have received the message that you are one of the helpers in the world. You may subconsciously believe you are the one who needs to take on the role of making everything and everyone better. You may feel guilty if you don't put others first and yourself last. Within your caregiver role, you become so focused on what is in front of you today that you lose sight of the energy and emotional health needed in the future as your role transitions into different stages, experiencing grief through these transitions and after your loved one's death. It becomes time to create a new life, knowing that you are no longer a caregiver. There are areas in your life you may have to put on hold to spend time reintroducing the things that bring you joy and purpose.

Does this sound familiar? Are you wondering why you tend to cater to others' needs over your own? Do you find yourself feeling exhausted, resentful of the attention your loved one receives while you are the one keeping their life running as smoothly as possible on a daily basis? Are you feeling invisible within the relationships that you had prior to your caregiving? While journaling, think back into your own life story to understand when these patterns were formed.

If you put others before yourself for so long, you may eventually become resentful. You might begin feeling a loss of self. You put so much energy into your loved one as you navigate their medical support team, advocating for their needs and wishes. Knowing that caregiving is only one aspect of your day, and your other responsibilities need your time and attention as well, if you are not aware of your values and Inner Purpose Feeling, you can find yourself in caregiver burnout. The loss of self creeps up, and suddenly, you may not know what makes you happy or what your hopes are for the future. It is important to spend time acknowledging the grief you need to move through and the changes occurring in your relationship with your loved one while the progression of their disease advances. For Example: *You are a spouse, transitioning to a caregiver. It is hard to maintain the separation of one and the other. There may be changes within your physical relationship and how you now need to communicate with your spouse. You may realize that the hopes and dreams you once had for each other have changed. Your loved one also may need to come to terms with their own reality of the progression of their disease, and you may not be able to help them through their personal anger or acceptance of their reality.*

Practicing daily journaling will support you to listen to your voice while finding clarity within this new practice. You will awaken to lessons learned to this point in your workbook, supporting you to move forward and experience confidence as you grow within your new awareness. This will create space for you to build more stamina to continue your caregiving role.

Arc of Intense Energy Reflection:

Refer to the diagram and description of the Arc of Intense Energy in Conversation 1. Reflect on the topic of this chapter – *Setting Personal Boundaries To Express My Truth*. Answer the following questions to understand how the *Arc* is showing up for you:

What is your old, automatic pattern when triggered? For example, *I did not learn to set boundaries in my life. I stayed silent, the good girl, not making waves. I did whatever was necessary to please those in my life regardless of how I felt or what I was giving away:*

What is a new behaviour, belief or attitude you would like to choose instead? For example, I have learned to set boundaries around how much I give of myself to others. I have learned to say No and I understand that it is not my purpose to make everyone happy. I can face conflict, and I now know that my needs and beliefs are important:

Practice self-managing through the *Arc* when you are learning about living true to your values. Begin by paying attention, noticing the energy or discomfort intensifying in the body. As this occurs, practice relaxing your shoulders and belly and deepen and slow your breathing.
This will allow you to feel the emotions as they arise, notice your thoughts and determine if they are aligned with your values or just old, unhelpful messages. Write about these emotions and thoughts in your journal.

When you learn to understand what is true and right, you will be able to articulate and understand how to respond to uncomfortable situations in life. While caregiving, you will feel intense emotions, but you will be able to determine where they are coming from and make decisions that serve both you and your loved one. For example, your *Arc* may be presenting from a place of personal fatigue or frustration within a caregiving situation.

By managing the *Arc* through journaling, you will be able to find a new self-awareness about what to do next while shifting old patterns and thoughts.

Action Steps

Reflections:

- What areas within your daily living could use boundaries? For example: *Within my caregiving role in the early stages of my husband's disease, it would have been helpful to set the boundary allowing me to take the vacation time from work that I was entitled to. I didn't take vacation time in case I needed time when my husband's disease progressed. Without setting that boundary I was not allowing myself time away from work and a more relaxed time at home, creating space for fun in my life:*

- What emotions and feelings that come up within your caregiver role do you need to communicate with others? For example: *When I felt overwhelmed and life was out of control, I kept these emotions and feelings to myself. I used to go down to my laundry room, turn on the dryer and cry and then wipe my tears and go on with what I needed to do. There were people in my life who would have stepped in to help or been there to listen but I was functioning from an old pattern that I had to be strong and do it all on my own:*

- What old patterns and thoughts around over-giving and not allowing time for yourself have you been experiencing? For example: *When I was caregiving, I was over-giving every day, but I was not aware I was. I was not awake to the possibility that I was giving to everyone and not to my own needs because that had been my pattern from childhood. I was doing it all; I was not going to be a failure. I was the good girl who keeps everyone happy. The expectations that I had set for myself were not realistic and could not be maintained. I learned that I could love and provide for my family without giving all of me. My husband and children, friends and co-workers did not judge me for what I could or could not do. This was a pattern and thought that was being told to me by my inner critic:*

- What small daily changes can you make to support your emotional, physical, and spiritual needs while maintaining your role as a caregiver? For example: *Initially, I started to set aside half an hour every morning with my morning coffee and a journal to write out my thoughts before the family got up to sit. I started to take the time to eat because I had been skipping meals. I would take a walk at lunch time because when I got home at night, I had my home/family responsibilities. I would take an hour, go to the library, sit in the silence and read, journal or just enjoy being alone with myself. I started slowly and had to let go of the guilt I felt because I had to focus on what I needed:*

- What new self-care routine would you like to implement? How do you feel these small changes will help decision-making and planning for the future?

Continued Daily Practices Supporting Setting Boundaries Through Journaling:

Review the foundational practices you have been committing to. If you feel comfortable with all of them, continue including them in your daily routine. However, if you are not resonating with one or more, take the time to discover what you prefer practicing to create a mindset that promotes physical, emotional, and spiritual presence. If you have too much going on, feel free to drop one to make space for rest.
Stick with the free-flow activities you have been enjoying. If you have space, feel free to add a free-flow writing after you have journaled once a week.

What's Next? Have a Conversation With Your Soul Through Journaling:

What is your soul saying to you about setting boundaries? How are you feeling about communicating boundaries now, and how can you express this through journaling – having a conversation with your soul? Grab your journal and write what you are discovering about yourself.

A Conversation With My Soul
By Donna Fitzgerald

Pain and Grief

You are never prepared for the death of the one you love. It is still a shock.

Although I had been preparing for his death for months, I was not prepared when he finally took his last breath. Me by his side with so many thoughts going through my mind, it was like "wait a minute, he always bounces back. I am not ready to say good-bye yet."

The next couple of weeks are a whirlwind of activity. Preparing for the funeral and helping our children cope with this loss in their lives. It's not fair that my children have lost their father at such young ages.

My son had the opportunity to look in his father's eyes briefly before he was medicated to help relieve the sense of suffocation. Our daughter did not have that opportunity to say good-bye to her father as she didn't like going to the hospital. We sat on my bed, and she wrote a letter to her father and decorated the envelope to say good-bye. She had me place it in the casket on the day of the funeral.

I was numb. I again was writing lists and planning all that needed to be done.

Months passed, and the grief at times was physically painful. I realized I was a single parent. There was no one to ask or talk to about having grieving children. I lost my best friend and husband.

How would I ever get through this pain? It was a pain I have not experienced before. I ask myself this question: How are you going to keep your kids from falling apart? My answer, falling apart is not an option.

I made some decisions. I had given up running and could barely get out of bed and get to work. It had been four months since I tied up my running shoes for a run. I joined a session at our local Running Room to get started again. It was time to get back on track.

Work was never the same after the meeting with my manager, not knowing what I had done wrong. I was told that my co-workers were complaining about my work. I understood that I had been caregiving for my husband for six years and that certainly affected the energy I had for work. In my head, I was giving 100% at work but it was giving 100% of what I had left. I felt it would be best to move on to a new job after one year. I was told not to make major changes for a year after a traumatic event.

I decided it was time to make a positive move out of a negative situation. I made a little handbook of what we experienced in the first year of living with ALS. I offered to volunteer at the Neuromuscular Clinic at the hospital where my husband spent the last 18 months of his life.

If I could help one family who was experiencing the emotional roller coaster ride of ALS, I had succeeded in my goal.

Within a year I put all these changes into place. I also decided to move again. The house we were in was a house that represented the last stages of ALS - my husband's frustration, anger, and our family exhausted. Life moves on and forward I go!

Navigating Transitions Toward The Future

Journaling Through Conversation 8
Part 1

Transitioning with self-awareness.

How can you move through caregiving while creating new awareness to support moving towards the future?

The following worksheet will support you to use your inner voice through journaling to navigate transitions and change, whether they are intentionally planned experiences or unforeseen occurrences. It will provide the awareness that transition becomes more comfortable as we accept our truth and welcome the wisdom of our soul into our life.

The worksheets up to this point have given you a new awareness of who you are and having daily conversations with your soul through your writing.

The following information and self-care practices will help support you to make decisions and changes that will feel more authentic and guided by your intuition. You will have new awareness to move through the emotions and feelings of managing the ongoing care of your loved one, grief through the death of a loved one, creating the space and time to create a new life after caregiving in a way that you hold their memory within you as you move forward. Making changes that create new experiences that bring new opportunities and growth.

Things to Consider About Navigating Transitions:

- Transitions can be uncomfortable, but they also provide the wisdom needed to personally evolve;
- There are three thoughts to consider regarding navigating transitions:
- Stop, Look, Listen;
- It is possible to move through the process of transitioning into the future in a different way than you planned.

Transitions can be uncomfortable, but they also provide the wisdom needed to personally evolve:

Transitions can be startling when you are not prepared for them or closed to the *not knowing* of life. If you have been programmed to be in control, the feelings experienced through change can range from exciting to mildly unsettling or even devastating. However, transitions can also be a time for new and meaningful opportunities to emerge, and for you to experience more personal awareness and wisdom.

It is said that *the only constant in life is change*, and in your life as a caregiver, this is a daily reality. Prior to your caregiving role you might not have been aware of the amount of changes happening in your life as you lived going through the motions and not fully awake to the importance of your inner health. You may have been experiencing life from the outside world, rather than the world that lives within you.

You can resist transition, remaining in grief and loss of self, or you can learn to accept your emotions and feelings and grow within yourself to listen to your inner voice to help understand and move forward within transition. If you make the choice to accept change, go with the flow and build the skills and capacity to navigate unforeseen transitions, you can reduce your stress levels and the amount of time and energy you spend worrying because you have new awareness, providing clarity and a sense of control. This then translates to being open to possibilities for the future that you may not have considered in the past. Your new self-awareness and stronger sense of self allows you to see life after caregiving and what new possibilities can be imagined.

There are three thoughts to consider regarding navigating transitions:

Here in Canada, when we were children learning how to venture into the unknown of crossing a busy street, we were given guidance that is equally applicable as we navigate change:

Stop, Look, and Listen:

- Stop and breathe: take the time to make space for transition in the *busy-ness* of your life and as you begin creating a new relationship with your soul;
- Look within: get to know yourself again and articulate what is truly important in your life and what you want for yourself;
- Listen to what arises: practice patience and listen to what bubbles up as you re-discover new awareness about yourself and old patterns of the past that have kept you from living more authentically.

Navigating Uncomfortable Transitions:

In September 1998, my husband was diagnosed with ALS at the age of forty-three. We had been married for eighteen years. We had moved into our dream home in the country that he built for our family one month before. Within a matter of weeks, we went from joy and excitement for our new home in the country to a diagnosis of ALS with a life expectancy of 3-5 years. The devastating news that no one survives ALS.

The next two years were extremely difficult. My husband was transitioning to a new life after leaving work and managing the changes in his mobility. He enrolled in a drug study in a city 3 hours away from our home. We wanted to do whatever we could to support research to find a cure. We made this trip once a month, and as the months passed, the amount of energy it took was becoming overwhelming. We dropped out of the drug study after a year because the travel was exhausting for both of us. We were still very hopeful and did what we could to raise money and awareness to find, if not a cure, a treatment to extend the lives of those with ALS. There was joy within these first two years with a trip to Florida to Disney that his co-workers sent our family on; our children were 5 and 12. My husband had time to spend with our children and to work around the house and property. I remained working to help support our family. We were trying hard to keep life as normal as possible.

During the next two years, transition moved in as ALS, and it was calling the shots. My husband was in a wheelchair full-time and needed around the clock care. We had homecare coming in a few times during the day while I was at work. Life had become a blur of things to do. I was my husband's primary caregiver from the time I came home from work until I left for work in the morning. It seemed that every week we were navigating and transitioning to a new stage of his disease. Our daughter was having nightmares from worrying, and her tummy was sore; I took her to counselling. I had a book in the kitchen that held our life: notes for when homecare came in, dates for medical and counselling appointments, and the kids' activities. We were still striving to keep life as normal as possible. We made it to every ball game, soccer game, and school event as a family. Although it took a great deal of planning, I had to transition into a different way of looking after the house because I remained working.

Work became my safe spot away from the caregiving. My co-workers hired a housekeeper to come twice a month, and it was such a gift to our family. I would come home to a clean house, and my husband didn't have to look at what needed to be done with him not having the ability to help out. Sunday became my cooking day. I spent the entire day in the kitchen to prepare meals for the week. My son could take meals out of the freezer and get them started before I got home to save time if there was an activity in the evening.

In the summer of 2002, my life changed forever, a transition that my husband and I weren't prepared for. I set expectations for myself that were not realistic. I made promises at the beginning of our ALS journey because I didn't know what ALS was and what it would take to care for my husband and family. I was exhausted from all the responsibilities in my life. I was not looking after myself. Where would I find the time? I was transitioning through so many emotions within my relationship with my husband and grieving the loss of us as husband and wife; losing our physical relationship, losing communication because he could no longer speak. I felt more like a caregiver than a wife, transitioning through my own emotions, fear, and reality, knowing my husband didn't want emotional support because he had me while working through his fear, changes, and stages of his disease. We were both trying to parent and navigate our children's needs. I was broken, exhausted physically, emotionally, and spiritually. I hit a wall, and it was the most terrifying place to be. Hello, caregiver burnout.

In the Fall of 2002, my husband and I decided that he would go into respite for a few weeks so I could sleep through the night and have time to rest, which I had not done in over two years. Unfortunately, the two weeks without the daily caregiving gave my body time to rest, but when it was time for him to come back home, my mind and body said, *no, you can't do this*. I had heart palpitations, anxiety, fear, and I intuitively knew that if I brought him back home, I would disappear and not be there for myself, my husband, or my children.

This was one of the hardest decisions for our family, and the transition was not easy. The thing about transitions is that, in the beginning, they can feel extremely difficult and wrong, but after the dust settles, it is the best decision. My husband moved to a long-term care facility, and his life opened up because he saw people every day; there was activity, and people knew him, and he made friends. At home, he was isolated and alone most of the day. Friends had stopped coming by because we lived in the country a half an hour away from the city. I was able to organize a schedule for family and friends to pick a day they would visit for a coffee in the evening from Monday to Thursday. It was so much easier for them; they could talk about their lives, and there was enough activity that there could be quiet without being awkward because my husband could not speak. I had the energy and quality of time when I brought him home on Friday night until Sunday night. We were rested, and we enjoyed family time and knew how precious it was to have this time together. He came to life; the nurses, staff, and residents became his family. As much as we both held on to keeping him home, his life came alive while in care.

In November 2004, another transition appeared that we knew was coming, but I was not prepared for it. We had setbacks in the past, and he always bounced back, but not this time. My husband died peacefully with me by his side. We left nothing unsaid and he died on his own terms with dignity and love surrounding him on his last day. I have learned that transition is a part of life and that knowing who I am and what brings me joy and purpose has made my life more beautiful. I have transitioned through the grief of my husband's death, rebuilding myself after caregiver burnout, becoming a single parent and raising our children, and creating a life for me that has meaning. I never take anything for granted because I know it can be taken away in a heartbeat. I am grateful for every day.

I have grown so much within who I am. Having daily conversations with my soul through journaling helps me navigate any challenge that life presents. I have a sense of gratitude that I have been given the life I have and would not change anything because I am the woman I am today because of my journey. I hold my husband within my heart that he guides his family and me to face each day with hope, humour, and gratitude.

Stop - take the time to make space for transition in the busy-ness of your life and as you begin reviewing your story:

- Our culture values busy as super-people are applauded. There may be times when you keep busy as a distraction to avoid the uncomfortable feelings that transitioning towards something you really want brings up. There is a paradox in times of transition – in order to go forward, you must first learn to slow…
- Slowing may mean learning to make space physically, emotionally, and mentally, in your very full life. Transitions take time and emotional energy and require creating the commitment to yourself to use your self-care tools to help you manage emotions and acknowledge them. This is when you can learn the history and patterns created in your life and learn how they were shaped;
- It can be helpful to take things off your to-do list in order to make space for that free-flow thinking that inspires the yearning for change, personal growth, and a more reflective mindset. It may mean choosing to let go of activities you are no longer passionate about, so you can prioritize those that provide you with real meaning and purpose. Making space for transition involves setting the boundaries discussed in Conversation 7 and reflecting on the inner balance you crave in Conversation 6. It also entails reviewing your values' feelings, your Inner Purpose Feeling, and your best self, as described in the Enneagram, to use them as guideposts while prioritizing self-care and foundational practices when entering a period of transition – this may be the first time for you.

Now that you have introduced daily journaling and have worked through the worksheets. You have been getting to know yourself more intimately, having conversations that at times surprise you and at other times reveal the sides of yourself you don't like to face. With this new awareness, you can follow your intuition when you are being drawn to something new or make a change to create a more balanced way of being.

You may find that your relationships are becoming more meaningful as you share more of your authentic self with others. You are being drawn to new people and creating new relationships with others that hold the same values and understanding. You can understand and work through emotions that come with letting go of relationships that no longer serve you; understanding that these relationships come to teach you more about yourself and you can be grateful for the time you spent with these people. You will realize that you will experience grief and loss within letting go of what no longer speaks to you. You may feel inspired to change your job, buy a new home, travel, try something new that you always wanted to do but thought you couldn't. You are likely looking at the world differently now, and you can welcome feelings of fear and uncertainty because you have the personal awareness and confidence to ask yourself the questions, *Is this an old pattern? What about this scares me?*

You can take a leap of faith that may introduce you to a new adventure in your life that you didn't even know you could have experienced because you chose to take a chance. The more of these personal successes you experience, the more confidence you gain to try new things and step outside your comfort zone. Even if they don't work out, you gain a sense of gratitude for the experience because if you don't try, you will never know. You have the choice to move on to the next intuitively guided path that appears in front of you.

Look within to get to know yourself again and articulate what is truly important in your life and how you want to live the rest of it:

- You receive specific things, experiences, and people in your life because of how you learned to see the world and live within it;
- When something about your world changes and your current ways of being no longer work for you, you receive a wake-up call and possibly recognize that something needs to shift for you to survive emotionally. You may experience the trauma of a divorce, the death of a loved one, or burnout from caregiving. You may receive unwanted health-related news that affects your daily living, a disease or accident that changes your mobility. You may near the stage of retirement and not know what your next chapter looks like. Or, you may lose your life partner and need to start over as a widow or widower. These are the times when you might begin asking yourself, *What is life really about? What is my purpose? What is next? What is the reason I am meant to be here on this earth? How do I move on?*
- Change provides the opportunity to look deeply within your life story and current way of living. It gives you pause to reflect on *who* you are and discover what is truly important to you, without the mask of ego and unhelpful patterns of ways of thinking about and responding to the world that no longer serve you. Transition provides the opportunity for you to choose to be who you are without our culture's *shoulds*. For example, *I should live life as I always have, I should stay in this job because it gives me security, I should stay silent because no one wants to hear what I have to say, I should not change because I will lose friendships;*
- Whatever the *shoulds* of your life are, can you imagine what it would be like to live without them, aligned with who you truly are?
- During transition, you not only change your surroundings or the people you hold close to you but you may also shift your way of being with a stronger sense of self and increased confidence. Through this process, there may be periods of time when *who* you are can become cloudy as you move forward tentatively and on shaky ground. It is when you are willing to turn your attention inward and ask, *Who am I?* when you truly commit to personal evolution;
- What can help is taking the time to relax into your authentic self by continuing to learn what the next layers or patterns of thought and behaviour need to be let go of. By letting go of assumptions about how life should be lived, new revelations are discovered about how you want to live moving forward. Self-awareness provides more of a choice when answering the question, What's next?
- Knowing that transition and change happens within the small daily changes and not all at once allows you the freedom to fall down and make mistakes. You can make changes you are not familiar with, being gentle with yourself as these are made;
- Spending time gathering information from friends and family to help you articulate who you are when at your best and what your unique gifts are as a human being provides deeper clarity about your values and vision for life. This adds a new layer of self-awareness that you may have not seen before. Once it is brought to your attention, you are able to journal and articulate what parts of you are celebrated by others that you were not aware of;
- This provides a fresh look at where you want to set different boundaries for what is acceptable and what is not. You can reflect on situations in your life where you may not be living congruently with your values;
- You can learn to integrate your thinking mind with your emotions and intuition, your soul. In your day-to-day life, you may be spending much of your time in your thinking mind and not being encouraged to follow your intuition. You might, metaphorically, cut yourself off from your body and the ability to

sense what is really going on. By slowing and integrating the head, heart, and body, you can become more mindful of bringing additional information to your decision-making. Your day-to-day way of being becomes more complete and allows you to live in the moment with who you are;
- With a guide or on your own, you are then able to welcome transition and do whatever it takes to move past the *shoulds* to see something different than you ever imagined. You feel an inspired knowing or nudge to move forward and a sense of excitement at the thought of what could be;
- As you look back on where you were within your caregiving journey and where you are now, you may not need to look for acceptance outside of yourself because you are now living in line with your values, your Inner Purpose Feeling, true to your authentic self. You have made changes to gain clarity and a connection within your soul, and life seems to flow more easily. You may feel less lonely because of the new relationship with your soul. You now know that you are never alone.

Listen to what arises: practice patience and listen to what bubbles up as you re-discover new life possibilities, as well as, awakenings as you review your life:

- Transitions take time and require patience in order to listen to the conversations your soul so desperately wants you to pay attention to. Developing self-awareness of your patterns around patience and impatience, as well as, developing compassion for yourself, can be helpful. Being open to what feels right takes you in an entirely different direction than when you try to force a way of being;
- Knowing that you are still providing care for your loved one and how important it is to you, allow the time and commitment to your new daily practices to regain a sense of who you are and your importance. Changes can be made to meet your needs and the needs of the others with thought and planning. You are creating a new way of being that speaks to your truth and is in line with your personal values and honours your Inner Purpose Feeling. You will be grateful for this new awareness as you move through transitions beyond caregiving;
- In addition, be open to asking for help from your community of support and commit to your foundational practices - nutrition, movement, fun, spirituality, and rest. If you feel it is helpful, use the growth and awareness you have experienced to seek outside support from a therapist, coach, mentor, or friend to help with any lingering grief and triggering emotions you experience.

Arc of Intense Energy Reflection:

Refer to the diagram and description of the Arc of Intense Energy in Conversation 1. Reflect on the topic of this chapter – *Navigating Transitions Toward The Future*. Answer the following questions to understand how the *Arc* is showing up for you:

What is your old, automatic pattern when triggered? For example, *I lived in fear and self-doubt. I didn't step outside my comfort zone to learn more about myself. I knew my roles and place in life at home and at work. I lived from a place of doing what I felt others expected or required of me:*

What is a new behaviour, belief or attitude you would like to choose instead? For example, *I no longer live in fear. I welcome fear and challenge it. I push myself to get outside my comfort zone in all areas of my life. I have come to welcome the lessons and growth that occurs when I don't let fear hold me back:*

Practice self-managing through the *Arc* when you are learning about living true to your values. Begin by paying attention, noticing the energy or discomfort intensifying in the body. As this occurs, practice relaxing your shoulders and belly and deepen and slow your breathing.
This will allow you to feel the emotions as they arise, notice your thoughts and determine if they are aligned with your values or just old, unhelpful messages. Write about these emotions and thoughts in your journal.

When you learn to understand what is true and right, you will be able to articulate and understand how to respond to uncomfortable situations in life. While caregiving, you will feel intense emotions, but you will be able to determine where they are coming from and make decisions that serve both you and your loved one. For example, your *Arc* may be presenting from a place of personal fatigue or frustration within a caregiving situation.

By managing the *Arc* through journaling, you will be able to find a new self-awareness about what to do next while shifting old patterns and thoughts.

Action Steps

Exercise:

Develop awareness of the specifics of your reaction to transitions and change:

The first step is becoming aware of how you react and think about transition or change. Complete the following exercise for the next four weeks:

- In your journal begin an on-going conversation once a week - an inquiry - a continuous intentional reflection about a topic with the process being more important than the end answer that emerges. Reflect on the following questions for ten minutes once a week. Answer all of them each time and notice the layers of awareness that arise. Reflect on what you learn about yourself and what you can do differently as a result;
- You may have chosen to use a specific journal while working through these worksheets Or, you may have a journal that you use for your daily morning journaling. In your journal, choose a different colour pen for each inquiry focusing on the topic of transitions. Write the date at the top of the page, answering the questions once a week. If you want to go back and look at your journal entries about moving through transition, you will be able to easily find your entry by the colour.

Inquiry Reflections:

- How do you feel about transition and change?

- What were you aware of about the transitions and change in your life in the past? Did you just roll with it?

- At the moment, describe how you are you open to making difficult decisions within your routine and responsibilities to live more authentically within transition and change. How are you allowing your inner critic to create an excuse for you not to act now? For example, *I feel judged by others when I take time to support myself. I may need to wait until my life is less hectic:*

- How would it feel to remain centered and clear in the wake of change and to be open to the emotions and feelings that come up?

- What are you noticing is different as you slow down and pay attention to your internal voice while having these conversations with your soul? For example, I made the necessary changes to create a safter environment for my husband and family with our decision to move him to a long-term care facility. However, I had to come to terms with the guilt I experienced because I broke another promise I made in the beginning stages of his disease:

- What are the ways you are taking care of yourself? Transitions take energy:

- As you continue to co-ordinate your daily self-care practices and routines, what are the steps you will take? For example, *I will get up an hour earlier every day to journal and meditate when the house is quiet as part of my self-care. I will also create a date with myself once a week to do something that brings me joy. I will walk an hour a day to move my body and be out in the fresh air and nature:*

- What beliefs and behaviors may be blocking you from seeing new possibilities for what is next?

- What support can you put in place as you navigate through this transition? For example. *I will ask friends or family for help to free up time to work on myself. I will rearrange my caregiver responsibilities to allow a bit more flexibility. I will hand off some of my responsibilities to others knowing there are people in my life who are waiting for me to reach out:*

- At the end of each week in your journal, make a list of how you spent your days - for each activity notice where your energy builds and where it drains. Ask yourself, *For the sake of what am I doing this activity?* Begin to notice what experiences are truly important to you and what it is about the activity that makes it so meaningful. Reflect on what you are learning and what you can do differently as a result. Write your reflections here:

Continued Daily Practices Supporting Navigating Transitions Through Journaling:

Review the foundational practices you have been committing to. If you feel comfortable with all of them, continue including them in your daily routine. However, if you are not resonating with one or more, take the time to discover what you prefer practicing to create a mindset that promotes physical, emotional, and spiritual presence. If you have too much going on, feel free to drop one to make space for rest.

Stick with the free-flow activities you have been enjoying. If you have space, feel free to add a free-flow writing after you journal a few times a week.

What's Next? Have a Conversation With Your Soul Through Journaling:

What is your soul saying to you about navigating transitions? How are you feeling about moving through change now, and how can you express this through journaling – having a conversation with your soul? Grab your journal and write what you are discovering about yourself.

A Conversation With My Soul

By Donna Fitzgerald

I Found Donna

I feel emotion welling up from within myself as I remember that fateful day 18 years ago that I sat looking blankly out into the water wondering. Where is Donna?

I found Donna and today I sit here experiencing memories of all the wonderful times we spent as a family at the lake swimming, fishing, campfires, playing cards, visiting with friends.

It is the first time I have been back to the cottages in over 10 years. It was too painful to come back to the lake where I realized I had lost Donna while trying to manage all my roles in life I had hit my breaking point, caregiver burnout.

Now so many years later I feel so grateful for these memories and there is no pain or grief. I have healed from the losses and emotions. I have grown and have been awakened to the strength I carry within myself to life my truly authentic life. I welcome the memories today and the tears that are coming to the surface. These are not tears of pain, regret, loss, they are tears of gratitude and love for these old memories that are here to remind me of all the laughter, love that my family experienced here.

I feel guided to write to my husband Cliff today.

Dear Cliff,

I am here on the dock at Palmerston Lake, you would love it here in the cabin and an area to swim. I can feel you within the wind as I write this morning alone on the dock by the water's edge.

I have cried happy tears this morning, remembering all the wonderful family times we spent here with the kids. It has been 10 years since I have been here and 18 years since I was lost and alone within myself. I sit her today so grateful for the life I have created. The two wonderful adults I have helped to shape and there is so much of you in them.

I think of our marriage and I had never felt that I was with the wrong person. I truly feel if you were still well we would be celebrating our 40th year of marriage as happy as I was the day we married and knowing I had found my wish of being a wife and mother when I was a 13 year old girl.

You my love, gave me this gift. I was your wife. I loved you with all my heart and soul. I stood beside you until your last breath. I know deep within my soul you would have done the same for me.

God had a different path for both of us. I was given the task of healing my past so I can give hope, compassion to others that find themselves lost, alone and afraid as I did so many years ago. God has a plan for me to be of service as we move into a new world post pandemic.

Through all the chaos I have been able to maintain a sense of calm and direction.

Cliff, I am listening to my inner guidance to move forward even when fear sneaks up on me. I have been preparing for this time in my life for the past 18 years, well really my entire life.

Cliff, God has given me my voice which I share through my writing and my way of being in my day-to-day life. To touch the lives of those seeking respite and growth. You my love have given me the strength and courage to have done all the work to move forward. If I feel unsure, I think of you and how strong and determined you were to stay with us. I take that strength with me every day and it helps me to move into my own destiny. Even after 16 years since your death you are still present in my life. Thank you for your love.

I have been brought here to the lake today a full circle moment at a wonderfully happy place for our family. I sit here today the woman I am in a large part because of your guidance, strength and teaching me of life's importance.

I have arrived! Thank you, Cliff for being part of my journey! I am not defined by my past. I am creating a future of love and light.

Love Donna.

After I wrote for quite some time. I closed my eyes and meditated and let the emotion and words move through my being. I opened my eyes and there was a monarch butterfly (Cliff). He gave me a butterfly necklace on our wedding day. I have always associated butterflies with him. The butterfly danced around me never landing but no more than three feet away. I started to cry and said thank you for acknowledging my words and my good-bye letter of the past knowing I have found Donna and I am living my best life without the pain, grief and loss of the past. I wiped my tears and started to make my way back up the stairs to the cottage. The butterfly followed me as I made my way to the top of the stairs until I sat down. Life has so many miracles and this is one I will hold close to my heart.

Envisioning The Life You Would Like To Create

Journaling Through Conversation 8
Part 2

Begin envisioning the life you would like to create.

How can you create a vision for your life after caregiving?

The following worksheet will support you in creating your new life vision through transformation. It is called a Vision Board and is broader than just emotions. It will also be a tool to compare with the Emotional Feeling Board you made in Conversation 2. You will be able to see and articulate the growth within yourself since moving through this series of worksheets and daily journaling practice to create your new awareness.

This visioning process will reveal what you feel subconsciously and may not be aware of. Along with your newfound daily practice of self-discovery through journaling, this art of reflective collage will help you articulate and find clarity about what your authentic future will look and feel like as you continue your new path of personal transformation.
It will naturally reveal things without you realizing it is happening.

Things To Consider To Experience Envisioning The Life You Would Like to Create:

- Move through the same process you did when creating your Emotional Feeling Board in Conversation 2;
- Gather items you need to create your board;
- Prepare a relaxing space that provides ease away from daily stressors;
- Move through a mindful, sensory process guided by your intuition, your soul;
- Review how you felt when you experienced your Emotional Feeling Board 6 weeks ago;
- Reflect on the awakenings that occur as you review your Vision Board;
- Interpret your reflections through your journaling practice;
- Summarize how you feel emotionally after moving through the process of creating and interpreting

your board.

Move through the same process you did when creating your Emotional Feeling Board in conversation 2:

- Your Vision Board will create the storyline for your future as you move through transitions and new awakenings and develop even more awareness over time;
- The purpose of the Vision Board is the same as the Emotional Feeling Board: to move forward to live a life more authentically and true to your soul;
- You will create a new collage with the same process as in Conversation 2. The difference this time is that you have completed weeks of inner work and experienced awakenings and growth within yourself;
- You have now connected with your emotions and feelings to have a new view of what makes you happy, what excites you ,and what your intuition nudges you to change in order to live a more authentic life;
- Take the time to relax with this collage and let your soul have fun!

Gather items you need to create your board:

- A canvas or poster board;
- A magazine; yes, just one! I prefer using an Oprah magazine as it is full of images, colours, and words;
- A glue stick or liquid glue;
- A sealer medium like Mod Podge; I prefer *matte* as opposed to *shiny*;
- Separate piece of paper and your journal.

Prepare a relaxing space that provides ease away from daily stressors:

- Put on your most comfortable clothing, finding a space that allows for the energy you need to create;
- Put your favourite music on – it may be easy listening, or it may be upbeat – play what inspires you, or no music at all if that resonates;
- Light a scented candle if this is something you enjoy or an unscented one for ambiance;
- Set your canvas or poster board on the table in front of where you will be sitting;
- Give yourself one hour to create your Vision Board.

Move through a mindful, sensory process guided by your intuition, your soul:

- Begin looking through your magazine, trusting your intuition as you choose images that resonate with you – avoid trying to justify why you are choosing them; it may be a colour or a memory that comes up, or an item you are drawn to, or it may be a series of words or phrases – decide only based on a positive emotional response you experience;
- Rip out images that resonate with you for whatever reason – pleasant or not, avoiding the use of scissors as they motivate perfectionism and detract from the sensory experience of ripping the paper – *feel* the paper and *listen* to it rip as you use the index finger of your non-dominant hand to guide the paper along while using your dominant hand to pull the paper up and around that finger;
- Put a dab of glue on the image and intuitively find a place directly on your canvas or poster board once ripped out – avoid making a pile of images to choose from later. Instead, place each on the spot on your board as soon as you choose it and rip it out of the magazine. Trust this process as it is based on how you feel and where the image is meant to be from the moment you place it down. Trust your emotions;

- Once you have gone through the magazine, flip through the pages once more to see if anything else resonates that you may have missed. Don't worry if your canvas or poster board is not completely filled as white space reflects emotions you may not have
- investigated yet or been curious about. Your board may end up having more images than words or vice versa, or it may have a combination of both;
- Write your name and the date on the back of the board, so you remember when you created it.

Action Steps

Exercise: Review how you felt when you experienced your Emotional Feeling Board:

- Once complete, go back to Conversation 2 and review what you learned about how you felt at that time - review your notes on the back of your board;
- Compare your emotions from just 6 weeks ago with how you feel today;
- Review the vision board you just completed, experiencing the somatic sensations that arise in your body and the emotional feelings that arise from your soul. Both of these responses reflect whether your images represent your authentic self or not. For example, *are you feeling at ease, or are you feeling anxious? If at ease, the emotions you are experiencing reflect your authentic self. If you are feeling anxious, you are likely on the Arc of Intense Energy. Take a moment to reflect on why this might be.*

Reflect on the awakenings that occur as you review your board:

Sit with a pen and your separate piece of paper and review what is revealed. What does your future look like? What does your new collage reveal? Has it changed significantly from your Emotional Feeling Board? Is there more clarity and direction? Are there subtle changes revealed within the images you chose? Write the date and what you feel as you experience your board. What do the themes and images represent? Were you drawn to a specific colour, phrase, or image? Why? Do you feel your board is expressing more about where you are now than you thought it would? For example, thoughts written on the back of my vision board in 2019:

A successful business that brings me joy and purpose every day.
My family and community are living in harmony.
I live life every day and have faith in the universe to guide me on my journey.
I am always growing and amazed at what is revealed along the way.
The amazing relationships in my life have been a gift to my heart.
My health of body, mind, and soul grows stronger every day.
My family is strong and loved. I am blessed

It is time to note how you feel emotionally today after all the work you have done to become more self-aware and live an authentic life. It is your vision as you find clarity about who you are now, within what you are experiencing at this moment. Did you find this second board to be a more creative and pleasant experience? Did it feel different from the first Emotional Feeling Board. For example, *I love the experience of creating both the Emotional Feeling Boards and the vision boards which I have continued to do once a year for the past 16 years. These boards have evolved over the years and depict where I was at the moment while giving me a window into my future as well. My values are always revealed within my boards, along with my subconscious hopes for my future in a way I never expect. Now, there is colour, joy, family, wellness, and purpose revealed in my boards. I can interpret the images I pick as they don't always literally express the meaning I have given to them.*

Reflections:

Interpret your reflections through your journaling practice:

This sample list of emotional feelings will help you as you interpret your vision board. You may feel an emotion arise that connects with a thought or memory while you journal your feelings, describing your collage.

Anger	Hope
Amazement	Insecurity
Confusion	Loneliness
Depression	Overwhelm
Disgust	Sadness
Excitement	Surprise
Fear	Trapped
Happiness	Uncomfortable
Helplessness	Worthless

Ask yourself the following questions as you reflect. Notice how it feels and what arises for you in terms of emotions and thoughts. Write down the interpretations you are experiencing in your journal.

- How do I feel right now?
- What do I notice about my thoughts?
- What emotions are arising?
- What was this experience like for me?
- What am I learning about myself as a result?

Notice how it feels to continue practicing being vulnerable within your journaling. How does it feel to commit to your daily practice of expressing yourself honestly and authentically through your journaling?

Creative Healing Through Transformation
2019

I have truly had fun with this new Vision Board sitting and thinking of what my new life would be like as I step into my dream of supporting others navigate their own challenges to become more connected to their own voices.

I think of more financial security for myself and my family. The ability to give back to the ALS Society in some small way with an annual donation to support caregivers.

I have cracked open the egg of creativity, and a new life is about to unfold. It will be messy at times. I welcome this as part of the journey. I am free-falling into the unknown and brave enough to take a leap of faith.

I will always strive to make a difference in my life and the life of those around me. I am feeding the souls are ask the questions, finding their own sense of self and purpose. This brings such joy, purpose, and gratitude into my life.

Continued Daily Practices Supporting Envisioning The Life You Would Like To Create Through Journaling:

Review the foundational practices you have been committing to. If you feel comfortable with all of them, continue including them in your daily routine. However, if you are not resonating with one or more, take the time to discover what you prefer practicing to create a mindset that promotes physical, emotional, and spiritual presence. If you have too much going on, feel free to drop one to make space for rest.

Stick with the free-flow activities you have been enjoying. If you have space, feel free to add a free-flow writing after each time you journal.

What's Next?

Continue having *Conversations With Your Soul* Through Journaling!
Find information about my programs at www.daringtoshare.com

CLOSING THOUGHTS
BY DONNA FITZGERALD

The year 2020 and a global pandemic inspired me to write this workbook. I am so proud to share Creative Healing Through Transformation: Conversations with my Soul with you. For many years, I journaled and contemplated writing a book about my journey through caregiving; moving through grief and creating a new life. When the pandemic hit, I found myself in the at-risk age category of over sixty, managing stay-at-home orders. I was so appreciative of my self-care routine I have come to value and cherish. This daily routine gave me a grounding space while the world outside my door was in chaos.

As the weeks moved into months, I began thinking of caregivers during this time and how support groups and access to medical services had changed and decreased. Meetings and contacts with physicians and health care professionals shifted to online or telephone calls. I remembered how isolated and alone I felt at times in my caregiving journey over sixteen years ago. I cannot imagine the stress with the COVID-19 layer added onto an already chaotic life.

I wondered what I could do to help caregivers from my home; how I could be of service to those who were searching for answers. As an author and Facilitator of Authentic Leadership Conversations™ with past experience volunteering within the caregiving field, it seemed like the perfect time to create a workbook with added personal writings to help caregivers reconnect with their soul. It would support them to listen to and process their fears using a tool from the comfort of their home while adding or creating a self-care routine to help them through difficult times.

With the help of Tana Heminsley and Diana Reyers, I was able to make this dream a reality. I am forever grateful for being able to collaborate with these wise and authentic women.

Over ten years ago, I worked through these worksheets. They awakened a part of me I didn't even know existed. Becoming more aware of my developed patterns and fears, I was able to ask myself the questions that help move me through life. I continue to revisit these worksheets and my daily ritual of journaling to find my sense of calm and peace. I certainly don't have life figured out, but I do know I am prepared for anything that life chooses to share with me.

By sharing Conversations With My Soul, my hope is that, along my journey, I will inspire others to start their personal journey. There was a time when I thought I would not heal, feel or even survive my daily reality. Through self-discovery and journaling, I have experienced personal growth and a new sense of confidence, and I enjoy every moment of my life. Life is not always easy, but I know how to evaluate and connect within myself in order to move through it with more clarity and ease.

This book is my legacy to my children. Life can be hard and sometime devastating, and when my husband passed away, I had a choice to make. I chose a commitment to live a more authentic life filled with joy. I am now retired, and my children are married, starting their own families. I have the privilege of being a Gramma while continuing to create to a life full of meaning and purpose. I welcome life and its lessons. I will never stop dreaming and challenging myself. I am excited to see what this next chapter of life brings me, and I wish you the same.

PRAISE FOR THE AUTHOR

It is said that 'when life gives you lemons, make lemonade'.
For the more adventuresome and extroverted, make margaritas.
But who actually makes the lemonade?
Who gets the lemons and cuts and squeezes them into the pitcher?
Who chooses the sweetener and figures out exactly how much to add?

I have known Donna for slightly less than a decade. Our relationship was initially professional, we were working colleagues and shared an office and so we got to know each other personally. Donna was the rock of the operation. If you needed something organized and followed through, she was the one to do it. Everyone came to her. She looked after everyone. I began to understand that she did that outside of work and for people who had major challenges in their lives. It was impressive, and a little daunting that she had that much incessant drive and compassion and that she always was so 'put together.'

Then I was let into the inner sanctum of her personal journey. Her marriage that was disrupted by her husband's illness. The care that she gave him to the very end. The challenge of raising two children at a time when they needed the attention of two parents when only one was available. Then her self-care strategies that she cultivated, a bit from despair but that grew into a new direction.

I have one short story that shows her character and tenacity. I was a triathlete. Donna was a runner. I asked her if she might like to join our swim group at the local pool. Of course, she was up for it but understandably a little nervous about how she would perform. After the first session, I asked her how it went and she said she struggled to make it to the end of the 25 meter pool. But she did and she liked the exercise and she liked the coffee with the group afterwards. About a year later, we were back in the office after a morning swim in which our coach gave us 10 X 200 meter intervals; that's 2 kilometers of swimming with a 10 second break every 200 meters. I asked how she found it; she said, 'I love 200s'. Of course she bought a bike and did the whole triathlon thing too.

Donna makes the most incredible lemonade, she chooses only the best ingredients, mixes them with love and care and shares it with any and all.

~ Michael O'Reilly, MD, Kingston, Ontario, Canada

ABOUT DONNA FITZGERALD

Photographer: Susie Lamont

Donna is a Facilitator of Authentic Leadership Conversations,™ co-author of Daring to Share There to Here, Volume 1 by Diana Reyers, and an active member of the Daring to Share Global™ team.

She volunteered with the Kingston Chapter of the ALS Society in Kingston, Ontario, Canada for eight years, providing support to families living with ALS. She received the *2007 – 2008 Volunteer Excellence Award* from ALS Ontario. Donna also volunteered with the Neuromuscular Clinic in Kingston, Ontario as a peer support volunteer. She was a volunteer with Hospice Kingston for two years as part of the Bereavement Support Program.

After being a caregiver to her late husband for six years as he battled ALS and passed away in 2004, Donna made a commitment to be of service to others. For the past sixteen years since her husband's death, she has volunteered in her community, supporting families and caregivers.

Donna has navigated grief, trauma, and loss of self within her personal healing process. Along with her professional expertise, she finds purpose sharing the tools and self-care practices that were instrumental in her healing while creating a new meaningful life.

Donna is now retired from the administrative assistant position she held for thirty-seven years. She enjoys spending time with her children, being a part of her one-year-old grandson's life, and loves being outdoors while tapping into her sense of adventure. Donna continues to offer support to those who find themselves wanting to heal and reconnect with their inner voice – to have meaningful *Conversations with Their Soul*.

PRAISE FOR THE AUTHOR

Tana has a unique presence that is gentle, yet also commanding. A phrase she has incorporated into her work, 'rigor and ease' describes her approach to her writing, her career and her life.
A remarkably accomplished woman, she leads with a
magnetism that draws people to her and her extensive body of work.
She has profoundly transformed the lives of so many through her wisdom, integrity, emotional intelligence and commitment to service.

She models 'rigor' through her many accomplishments. She earned her Executive MBA from Simon Fraser University. Her career has provided her with experience and insights into being a corporate executive and an entrepreneur. She owned a retail clothing store, was a member of BC Hydro's executive team, and is the founder of Authentic Leadership Global, Inc. – a business that supports coaches and organizations in building healthy, sustainable businesses. An accomplished coach herself, she was the recipient of the International Coach Federation Vancouver Chapter 2016 Coach Impact Award.

She is a prolific writer, publishing her first book "Awaken Your Authentic Leadership – Lead with Inner Clarity and Purpose" in 2013. She has gone on to publish two more books, "Awaken Your Authentic Leadership – Authenticity Journal" and "Authentic Leadership Conversations for Meaningful Connection." The books are the culmination of years of leading and coaching, sharing her research, her insights and her practices with hundreds of clients.

And yet, she models ease. Her presence is calming; she practices mindfulness, meditation, yoga and appreciates the beauty in life.

~ Laura Mack, CEO, Authentic Leadership Global™ Inc.

ABOUT TANA HEMINSLEY

Photographer: Sabrina Desjardins

Tana is an Author, the Founder of Authentic Leadership Global™ as well as a retired, award-winning Leadership Coach.

She was awarded the *Vancouver Charter Chapter of the International Coach Federation's 2016 Coach Impact Award*. In 2019 she received the *CEO Magazine's Business Consultant Award* and was a *Book Excellence Awards Finalist* for her second book - *Awaken Your Authentic Leadership - Authenticity Journal*.

Tana has published three books in the *Awaken Your Authentic Leadership* series - about how to be your best self as an organizational leader. She has also written her first book for a br*oader audience titled E*ASE Amidst Challenging Times: Simple Practices for Inner Peace Beyond COVID.

She has spoken to audiences at hundreds of engagements and was a keynote speaker at the 2018 China Executive and Leadership Coaching Summit in Beijing.

Tana has more than 35 years of business and leadership experience, is a thought-leader in the area of Authentic Leadership and Emotional Intelligence and has been researching and practicing mindfulness for more than 15 years.

Tana lives in beautiful British Columbia, Canada, with her husband, Chris and cat, Buddy.

THE HISTORY OF AUTHENTIC LEADERSHIP GLOBAL™

I've always enjoyed connecting people and building community.

The *Authentic Leadership Conversation™ Dinner Series* began in 2006 when I left my corporate job as an executive and became an integral leadership coach.

I wanted a way to offer clients a place where they could experience authenticity while learning about themselves, as well as develop their ability to be authentic and built a community of support.

I was delivering retreats and I remember one new mom, who was a colleague, saying to me over tea, that she couldn't take that much time away from her family and yet she wanted to participate in a program. I asked her what her wish list was – what she wanted to talk about, how she wanted to gather with others, and how often.

The first *Authentic Leadership Conversation™ Series* was born.

I started it for women leaders initially, and we had surprisingly rich conversations over fabulous dinners in beautiful restaurants in downtown Vancouver, B.C. For the first series, I wrote each topic before the next event, shared it in all of my nervousness with participants, and then made any final changes. I wrote a total of nine topics to begin with and added to them over the years.

I then began to offer a co-ed series for the public, as well as by-invitation-only sessions for both senior leaders and human resource professionals. I conducted them in face-to-face groups, on conference calls, and, eventually, via skype, Webex and Zoom. I learned that once people got used to technology, the level of rich conversation was remarkable, even with others who they had never met before that session.

In 2007, one of my clients from the dinner series, asked me to come and work with his team. For four years, I facilitated lunch and dinner series with small groups of his team members. I also provided coaching for his leadership team as a group and with individuals. I shared the *Authentic You™ Personal Planning System* with them as a way to support them to develop their authentic leadership.

Since 2009 myself and my friend and colleague, Laura Mack, have been training coaches and facilitators around the world delivering the *Authentic Leadership Conversation™ Series*, as well as several other Authentic Leadership programs for their clients.

In 2017, one of the members of the team from 2007 who was now a senior leader in the federal government called and said she had been using the Action Worksheets for all the years since we worked together initially, that we should be proud of the conversations and that it was *just what was needed for the next generation of leaders*. For a year and a half, we supported her by training facilitators and trainers of facilitators, as well as, facilitating a series of the conversations for her team.

In 2019, we were honored to receive the *CEO Magazine Award for Management Consulting* and the results we were supporting our clients to achieve.

BIBLIOGRAPHY

Following is a bibliography of books and resources that contributed to this work:

Carlson, Richard, and Joseph Bailey. Slowing down to the Speed of Life—How to create a more peaceful, simpler life from the inside out. New York: HarperCollins Books, 1997.

Effects of Stress, http://www.webmd.com/balance/stress-management/stress-management-effects-of-stress

George, Bill. True North – Discover your Authentic Leadership. San Francisco: Josey Bass, 2007.

George, Bill, and Peter Sims, Andrew N. McLean, and Diana Mayer. "Discovering Your Authentic Leadership." Harvard Business Review, Volume 85: No 2 (February 2007), 129 - 138.

Goleman, Daniel. "What Makes a Leader?", Harvard Business Review, http://hbr.org/2004/01/what-makes-a-leader/ar/1, 1998.

Heminsley, Tana. Awaken Your Authentic Leadership – Lead with Inner Clarity and Purpose. Vancouver: Authentic Leadership Global,™ Inc. – Publishing Division.

Lerner, Harriet, Ph.D. The Dance of Anger – A Woman's Guide to Changing the Patterns in Relationships. New York: Harper & Row Publishers, 2005.

Reyers, Diana and Heminsley, Tana. Daring To Share Your Story: An Authentic Writing Guide. Canada: Daring to Share Global™, 2021, 28.

Riso, Don Richard and Hudson, Russ. The Wisdom Of The Enneagram: The Complete Guide to Psychological and Spiritual Growth for the Nine Personality Types.

IN MEMORY OF CLIFFORD THOMAS FITZGERALD

1955 - 2004

www.ingramcontent.com/pod-product-compliance
Lightning Source LLC
Chambersburg PA
CBHW081507080526
44589CB00017B/2685